Secrets FOR
Successful
LIVING

Secrets *FOR* Successful *Living*

JOHN E. FELLERS

DIMENSIONS
FOR LIVING

NASHVILLE

SECRETS FOR SUCCESSFUL LIVING

Copyright © 1993 by Dimensions for Living

93 94 95 96 97 98 99 00 01 02 — 10 9 8 7 6 5 4 3 2 1

This book is printed on acid-free recycled paper.

Library of Congress Cataloging-in-Publication Data

Fellers, John E. (John Eugene), 1935–
  Secrets for successful living/John E. Fellers.
    p. cm.
  ISBN 0-687-37133-3 (pbk.: alk. paper)
  1. Christian life—1960– . 2. Success—Religious aspects—Christianity. I. Title.
BV4501.2.F43   1993
248.4—dc20   92-38711

Scripture quotations are from the New Revised Standard Version Bible, Copyright 1989 by the Division of Christian Education of the National Council of the Churches of Christ in the USA. Used by permission.

The poem "I am God's Child" on p. 21 is from *Self Esteem: The New Reformation,* © 1982 by Dr. Robert H. Schuller, published by Word, Inc., Dallas, Texas. Used with permission.
  "Credo," pp. 38-39, is from *All I Really Need to Know I Learned in Kindergarten* by Robert Fulghum, Copyright © 1986 by Robert Fulghum. Reprinted by permission of Villard Books, a division of Random House, Inc.
  The poem on page 71 is an excerpt from *Markings* by Dag Hammarskhold, trans. L. Sjoberg & W. H. Auden. Translation Copyright © 1964 by Alfred A. Knopf, Inc. and Faber & Faber, Ltd. Reprinted by permission of Alfred A. Knopf, Inc., and Faber & Faber of London.

MANUFACTURED IN THE UNITED STATES OF AMERICA

To my children,
Stephanie, Eugenia, Terri, and Larry

* * *

With a special word of appreciation to
my friend, colleague, and brother in ministry,
The Reverend Robert L. Burgess

Contents

CONTENTS

Finding Out
Who You Are

Searching for
Personal Identity

Hollywood once made a movie about an obscure but fascinating bit of history. The story began in the cataclysmic events of the Russian Revolution. In October 1917, food riots broke out in St. Petersburg. A few days later the Imperial Navy mutinied, and by the end of the month, Czar Nicholas II had abdicated. He and his family were immediately placed under house arrest, but soon were taken to first one and then another isolated location in the heart of Russia. After months of being shuttled from place to place, the Romanovs ended up in the small provincial town of Yekaterinburg. On a mid-summer night in July 1918, Nicholas, his wife, only son, and four daughters were herded into the basement of the house where they were imprisoned and machine-gunned to death.

A few years later, a beautiful young woman surfaced in Paris, claiming to be the Grand Duchess Anastasia, the only surviving daughter of Czar Nicholas. She insisted she had miraculously escaped the massacre and had come to Paris to join the other refugees who had fled the revolution.

In the movie version of this story, the Grand Duchess was played by Ingrid Bergman. As the plot unfolded, Anastasia was welcomed by many displaced Russians who desperately wanted to find a survivor of the imperial family. Others were more skeptical, convinced that the woman was an imposter being used by a clever group of charlatans to get their hands on the Romanov fortune, hidden away in the vaults of Swiss banks. The skeptics were almost certainly right; Anastasia did not survive the slaughter of her family. Recent evidence has been uncovered that the Czar's entire family was massacred, so the young woman who turned up in Paris was a fraud. But whoever she was, it is certain she was searching for an identity.

Each of us, at some point in our life, goes through an identity crisis, usually when we are making the transition from adolescence to adulthood. That is the time in life when we decide on a career, look for a mate, establish spiritual values, and set patterns for the future. However, our search for identity is never quite finished. Sometimes the trauma of a job change, the loss of a mate, a broken relationship, a spiritual problem, or a moral lapse causes us to question who we are. We find ourselves back at "square one," trying to establish a sense of selfhood.

Late one evening when I was reading my Bible, I happened to turn to the first few verses of Paul's letter to the Romans. They begin with the words, "Paul, a servant of Jesus Christ, called to be an apostle, set apart for the gospel of God" (1:1). In a flash of insight, I saw those words as I had never seen them before; here was a man who had a strong sense of himself.

In ancient times people did not begin letters with the simple salutations you and I use. I usually begin letters to my congregation with, "Dear Friends." During the first century, letters opened with an elaborate self-portrait of the author, as if the person were establishing his or her credentials. Paul followed this pattern and drew a clear, concise picture of himself. He knew who he was: "a servant of Jesus Christ," "an apostle," and "one set apart for the gospel." As I read and reread those words, I wondered what pattterns they might provide for helping people establish their personal identities in our own time. I found several.

Learn something about your origins.

Each of us needs to know where we came from, the influences that shaped us, and the forces that made us what we are. One way to begin is to learn something about our name. Several years ago I met a man with the same last name I have. Since there aren't a lot of "Fellers" in this country, we began to compare notes and decided we were distant cousins. My new "relative" asked if I knew much about my family's history, and I confessed I did not. A few months later, he dropped by my office with a fascinating explanation about the origin of our name.

It is German and means "keeper of furs." My curiosity was aroused, so I did some research about other names on my family tree. I discovered one name that means "a clear lake" or "clear stream." Another combines some German words which mean "one who grows grain." After a while I was able to piece together some probable information about my family: My ancestors were trappers who lived near a clear lake or stream and eventually married into a tribe of farmers. They were not royalty or aristocrats—just average, ordinary folks who worked hard to make a living.

Another way to find out about your origins is to explore your relationship with the whole human family. Thornton Wilder's play *Our Town* contains a profound bit of dialogue at the end of the first act. Two of the characters are discussing a get-well note a friend had received from her pastor. It arrived with an unusual address:

> Jane Crofut; The Crofut Farm; Grovers Corners; Sutton County; New Hampshire; United States of America; Continent of North America; Western Hemisphere; the Earth; the Solar System; the Universe; the Mind of God.

This address says a lot about Grovers Corners, Sutton County, and the Crofut Farm—but it says a great deal more about Jane. Her pastor was reminding her that she lived in a special relationship with God. He was echoing the biblical affirmation, "In him we live and move and have our being" (Acts 17:28).

Psalm 8 describes this relationship in some magnificent lines, which establish the parameters of the way we relate to God:

> What are human beings that you are mindful of them,
>   mortals that you care for them?
> Yet you have made them a little lower than God,
>   and crowned them with glory and honor.
> You have given them dominion over the works of your hands;
>   you have put all things under their feet. (Ps. 8:4-6)

Those words provide the best explanation of our origins that any of us could find. Each of us, with our flaws and failures, mistakes and shortcomings, was created by God. Our glory is not in our family tree or a genealogical chart, nor is it in our genes and chromosones. Our glory is our indestructible relationship with God, who made us in his image and touches us with the power of his love. Our identity finds its highest meaning when it is projected against the backdrop of God's creative purpose.

Come to grips with your humanness.

To be a human being means to be aware that we are a mixture of contradictory emotions, attitudes, and feelings. A graphic but realistic explanation of human nature was written by Edward Sanford Martin, in a poem called "Mixed":

> Within my earthly temple there's a crowd;
> There's one of us that's humble, one of us that's proud,
> There's one that's broken-hearted for his sins,
> There's one that, unrepentant, sits and grins;
> There's one that loves his neighbor as himself,
> And one that cares for naught but fame and pelf.
> From much corroding care I should be free
> If I could determine which is me.

The truth is that none of us knows which we are—each of us is a curious mixture of good and bad, right and wrong, lofty motives and base desires.

William Golding wrote his parable about human nature in *Lord of the Flies*, a story about some English choirboys marooned on a remote island without adult supervision. At a glance, no human being seems more innocent than a youngster who sings in a choir, has a clear treble voice, and looks like an angel dressed in a ruffled collar and colorful robe. Nevertheless, choirboys are human, like the rest of us.

In Golding's story, when the boys arrived on the island, they tried to establish a social order. But the structure soon fell to pieces and the boys began to act like savages. They armed themselves with weapons, slaughtered an animal in a ceremony reminiscent of an ancient pagan rite, and eventually killed one of the most decent members of the group, a chubby, good-natured lad who wore thick glasses and was nicknamed Piggy.

The youngsters were finally rescued, but they were never the same after their self-inflicted ordeal. Golding ends his book on a sad, somber note, as one of the characters weeps for "the end of innocence, the darkness of man's heart, and the fall through the air of the true, wise friend called Piggy."

But there is another side of human nature that should not be ignored. The Roman Catholic Church recently beatified a priest named Maxmillian Kolbe, whose story is an incredible testimony to the decency of the human spirit.

Father Kolbe was thrown into a cencentration camp because of his outspoken opposition to Hitler and the Nazi regime. During his captivity he struck up a friendship with a young Polish patriot. When the young man was summoned to the gas chambers, Kolbe insisted upon taking his place. He gave his own life so that his friend could live, and that man did in fact survive the horrors of the camp.

Which is the most honest assessment of human nature—the story of the choirboys, or the sacrifice of Father Kolbe? The answer is both—"Within my earthly temple there's a crowd." Each of us is a curious mixture of sinner and saint. The church has made much of *original sin,* but has neglected the strain of *original righteousness* that is also present in the human heart. Even the best of us can sin, and even the worst of us can accomplish good.

I once heard a man make a public confession about a serious moral lapse. There were tears and promises to start

13

over and do better. But the moment of truth came when he said, "I guess I forgot I was human."

Affirming our humanness, in all its grandeur and despair, is crucial to finding out who we are. If we deny this humanness, we are denying a part of ourselves. If we affirm it, we have taken an important step toward establishing our selfhood.

Discover your role.

While living in Houston, I served on the board of directors of a hospital in the Texas Medical Center. People from all over the world come there for treatment. Since the hospital is on the frontier of medical research, administrators often arrange for physicians pioneering in certain fields of medicine to come to board meetings and talk about their work. One of the doctors who spoke to us was Michael DeBakey, the famous heart surgeon.

I have never seen an individual so totally absorbed in his role. During one presentation, he talked about how miraculously by-pass surgery can improve a heart that is not functioning normally. Dr. DeBakey explained how such surgery can give a patient another chance to live an active, healthy life. I sat spell-bound while he described the procedure.

After one of Dr. DeBakey's presentations, I thought about how he had become the great humanitarian and healer he was. Late one afternoon, as I was making calls, I saw him striding through the corridors of the hospital with a group of students in tow. He was totally absorbed in his role as doctor and teacher. It was apparent that he had developed his God-given skills to their full potential. He was adventurous and creative. He was not afraid to step out on the frontier of healing to chart a new course. He believed in himself enough to be innovative. Medicine has not been the same since Michael DeBakey appeared on the scene.

All of us need this kind of strong, healthy, understanding of who we are and what we do, if we are to discover our own unique role in the grand scheme of things. And we need this sense of personal identity, not only in our careers, but in matters of the spirit as well.

Mother Teresa is one of the spiritual giants of our time. I have heard that her work began with a dream in which she was convinced that God was telling her to build an orphanage. When she informed the superior at her convent that God had told her to build an orphanage, the Mother Superior asked Teresa how much money she had. When the reply was "three pennies," the superior asked her what she expected to build with three pennies. It is said that Teresa replied, "With three pennies and God, I can build anything!"

Teresa went to India, where she did build an orphanage, a hospice for the dying, and medical clinics in the slums of Calcutta. Later she opened a center for AIDS victims in New York. When Mother Teresa was presented the Nobel Prize in 1979, she told the press that the most insidious disease that can prey on a human being is the feeling of not being wanted. She did not think that terrible disease could ever be cured, but there will always be loving hearts and willing hands.

This may be the secret to finding out who you are—living with hands anxious to serve and a heart ready to love.

Narcissus Is More Than a Flower

Developing a Healthy Self-image

One of the saddest stories in Greek mythology is about a character named Narcissus. He was very handsome—perhaps the most beautiful creature who ever lived—but his good looks were his downfall. Before Narcissus was born, a seer had told his mother that he must never be allowed to see his own face. But when the goddess Echo fell in love with him, Narcissus could not resist the temptation and looked at his reflection in a pool of clear water. From that moment, spurning the affection of Echo, he loved only himself.

Narcissus was so attracted to himself, says the legend, that he pined away and died. The gods realized they had made a mistake in creating someone so handsome, so they named a flower in his memory. These flowers often grow by a pool of water, much like the place where Narcissus died.

Psychoanalysts have referred to this story to describe a mental illness called *narcissism*. The disorder is a love of oneself so pervasive and consuming that it destroys all other relationships. A narcissistic person is focused almost entirely inward, so he or she cannot understand the needs of others or accept love from the people around them.

When we start exploring ways to develop a healthy self-image, many of us become frightened of the specter of narcissism. Narcissus is more than a flower when it becomes an emotional sickness. Nevertheless, everyone needs a positive self-image to be a functional human being. One of the crucial ingredients in successful living is to develop an adequate sense of self-esteem without becoming egocentric.

When Paul penned his letter to the Romans, it is doubtful whether he had ever visited there. Yet he knew that human nature is the same, regardless of where people live. Paul also understood some of the basic dynamics of human personality, and he had a good measure of common sense. He warned his readers: "I say to everyone among you not to think of yourself more highly than you ought to think, but to think with sober judgment, each according to the measure of faith that God has assigned" (Rom. 12:3).

Paul then describes a variety of gifts that different people enjoy. Since he was writing to a group of Christians, he lists a series of spiritual gifts, but moves beyond these to talk about life in general. Though Paul would never have thought of himself as a psychologist, he gave some profound advice about how to be a well-adjusted, whole person, at peace with God and with oneself. In the process, he sets down some guidelines for developing a healthy self-image.

If you analyze Paul's advice and translate it into your own life setting, you will discover several steps that will help you build a positive self-image.

Erase negative images of yourself.

Unfortunately, a lot of people become weighed down with negative images received when they are children, and they carry them into adulthood. No doubt you are aware of what will happen to a healthy arm or leg if it is kept bound and immobile for a few months, and never exercised. When the limb is loosened, it will be weak and almost paralyzed. The same thing can happen to the entire body. Go to bed for a week when you are perfectly healthy, then see how you feel seven days later. When you get up, you will barely be able to stand. Just a short walk around the room will exhaust you; you will be weak and dizzy, and in a few minutes, you will want to get back in bed.

17

The same thing can happen to our self-esteem. If we are told often enough that we are stupid, chances are, we will not learn. If we are told we are ugly, there is a strong possibility that we will lose all interest in our personal appearance. Tell a boy he is awkward, clumsy, or a poor athlete, and you can almost guarantee he will not compete in sports. Call a girl a wallflower, and before too long she will become antisocial and withdrawn.

It is unfortunate that many people have received messages like these at some point in their lives—from their parents, brothers and sisters, teachers, or friends. You may be one of them. The first step you need to take toward building a healthy self-esteem is to blot out these images and start listening for some positive feedback about yourself.

A young man named Roger worked on the staff of a large church. He was an effective minister, but there was one thing he would not do—sing. Roger never joined the congregation in singing hymns because he was too embarassed to try.

One day when the senior pastor asked why he refused to sing, Roger related an incident that had happened years before. When he was in third or fourth grade, his class was asked to sing for a school program. His teacher wanted the group to make a good impression, so she rehearsed the class diligently.

One day she heard some sour notes, and in a moment of impatience, she put the off-key youngsters in the back of the room and said, "Those in the back of the room are sparrows. You children in the front are my song birds." The teacher did not mean to be insensitive, but Roger never forgot what she said, nor did he ever again try to sing.

Fortunately, the senior pastor asked Roger to talk with the minister of music. It turned out that the young man did not have an accurate image of himself—he was not tone deaf, and he could sing as well as the average person. Roger did not leave the ministry to pursue a career in opera, but he soon learned to enjoy singing in church.[1]

Do you have negative images lurking in your psyche? If you do, you should erase them today. Getting rid of your feelings of inferiority, inadequacy, and insignificance is the first step toward developing a healthy image of yourself.

Take a realistic look at yourself.

A few years ago, Elizabeth Taylor's book, *Elizabeth Takes Off,* turned out to be a best seller. At first glance, this book seems to offer advice on how to shed pounds by dieting; but it is really about more than what to eat or how much you should weigh. The copy on the dust-jacket explains its real message:

> "Elizabeth Taylor . . . generously shares what she's learned . . . to encourage others to achieve the redoubtable energy that comes with winning back your self-esteem" (G. P. Putnam's Sons, 1987).

Miss Taylor explains that the "winning back" process started with a hard look at herself. One morning she looked in the mirror, and instead of seeing the beautiful star the world sees, or the talented, gifted person she thought she was, she saw a woman who was destroying herself with drink, drugs, overindulgence, and unhealthy relationships. That was a devastating moment of truth. She later wrote, "I had actually tossed away my self-respect. I had taken my image and scratched it with graffiti. I had thrown my gift away. . . . I was no longer even Elizabeth Taylor, the person I knew" (p. 48). That must have been a painful moment, but it was the beginning of her long climb back to self-worth.

Most of us have not had the problems with which Miss Taylor has had to cope. Nevertheless, we all share one thing in common: We can build a healthy self-image only when we have the honesty to look at ourselves as we really are. Until we do this, we have tossed away our self-respect and thrown away our gifts. When you find the courage to see yourself as you really are, you will have taken a giant step toward building a positive self-image.

19

Work with your potential.

Most of us use only a fraction of our physical and mental resources. Those who study human personality tell us there are great reservoirs of strength within every human being, waiting to be tapped.

Everyone has limitations, things we cannot do because we have not been trained to do them, or because we do not have the stamina or talent. I cannot ice skate, play professional football, or read music. But for all my limitations, there are many things I can do, and if I try hard enough, I can do them well.

One of the most popular artists in Japan is a man named Yoshikiko Yamamoto, who works in the medium of wood-block prints. His is a fascinating story. When he was six months old, his parents learned he had hydrocephalus—fluid on the brain. Doctors advised that their son would be severely retarded, and their predictions proved accurate. Yoshikiko's IQ has never tested higher than forty-two.

But Yoshikiko's parents loved their son and wanted him to enjoy life as much as he could. They put him in a special-education class where he learned to copy letters and write his name. He also learned to draw, and one day he turned in a beautiful sketch of a famous castle. His teacher saw his latent talent and urged him to concentrate on making wood-block prints. Eventually, he entered some of his work in a contest and won first prize. Soon his work began to sell, and today Yoshikiko Yamamoto, with his limited IQ, is a famous artist who is self-supporting and enjoys a well-ordered existence.

Someone who knows his situation well commented, "Rather than being obsessed with his limitations, he has capitalized on his potential."[2] This is one of the most crucial lessons we must learn in our search for self-esteem. We can feel good about ourselves when we face up to our limitations, accept them, and then work with the talents we have.

Remember—you belong to God!

Sometimes I become discouraged, just like everyone else. I feel that nothing is working out right, I am not living up to my

potential, and I may end up a failure. When I feel these
negative thoughts overwhelming me, I read a poem I
discovered several years ago:

> I may be young; I may be old,
> But I am somebody,
> For I am God's child.
> I may be educated; I may be unlettered,
> But I am somebody,
> For I am God's child.
> I may be black; I may be white,
> But I am somebody,
> For I am God's child.
> I may be rich; I may be poor,
> But I am somebody,
> For I am God's child.
> I may be fat; I may be thin,
> But I am somebody,
> For I am God's child.
> I may be married; I may be divorced,
> But I am somebody,
> For I am God's child.
> I may be successful; I may be a failure,
> But I am somebody,
> For I am God's child.
> I may be a sinner; I may be a saint,
> But I am somebody,
> For Jesus is my Savior,
> I am God's child![3]

This is the ultimate secret to helping build a healthy
self-image. This positive image is not an outgrowth of our
natural gifts and graces, our intellect or good looks, our
accomplishments or achievements; it is the inevitable result
of a trusting, loving, growing, adventuresome relationship
with God. Our self-esteem grows when we see ourselves as
God sees us, created in his image, wearing the imprint of his
glory.

If you visit New Orleans, be sure you go to the French
Quarter and see the building near the Mississippi River,
where slaves used to be sold. Most of the men and women

who were put on the auction block there were broken and defeated. But one day, there was a man waiting to be sold who stood tall, his head erect and his pride intact.

Someone asked, "Who is that fellow? Is he the straw boss, or does he own the slaves?"

"No," came the reply, "he's neither; he's a slave like the rest, but that fellow can't get it out of his head that he is the son of a king!"

Narcissus is more than a flower—it is a dangerous, insidious disease of the mind and spirit. An inferiority complex is also a harmful and debilitating emotional illness. But a positive self-image, a strong sense of self-worth, an honest confidence in ourselves, is the inalienable right of every child of God. None of us should think so highly of ourselves that we are consumed with love of self, but each of us should believe in ourselves as much as God believes in us!

What Does God Look Like?

Building a Personal Relationship with God

A little girl was drawing a picture during Sunday school. When her teacher asked the child what she was drawing, the little girl replied, "I am making a picture of God."

The teacher, conditioned by years of listening to sermons about an invisible God, responded, "But my dear, how can you do that? Nobody knows what God looks like."

The child answered, "When they see my picture, they will!"

There is a beautiful story at the beginning of Matthew's Gospel that tells about three individuals who found God in a face-to-face encounter (Matt. 2:1-12). We often read about them during the Christmas season. They are the "wise men," and we sometimes call them the Magi. We do not know much about them; tradition says they were astronomers from Persia who had traveled many miles to pay homage to a baby born in Bethlehem.

The arrival of these exotic visitors, with gifts fit for a king, is fraught with symbolism. Gold, frankincense, and myrrh—each provides a clue to the events in the life, ministry, death, and resurrection of Jesus. But the underlying message in this beautiful story is about the way God is revealed to us. There are moments in our lives when we see God face to face, and these encounters help us establish a personal relationship.

Such encounters provide a fascinating insight into the

story of the little girl, her picture, and her Sunday school teacher. Nobody knows what God looks like, so nobody can draw a picture of God—chalk one up for the teacher. But the little girl was closer to the kingdom of heaven than we might think—wherever and however we discover God, we meet God in a personal relationship, which means that God comes to us wearing a human face.

We see the face of God in Jesus.

The entire New Testament is an affirmation of something Jesus said: "Whoever has seen me has seen the Father" (John 14:9b). Sounds simple enough, but the church spent hundreds of years trying to explain how this could be possible. One explanation was written at the Council in Nicea, in A.D. 325, when theologians and bishops attempted to define how the Son was related to the Father. The result was the Nicean Creed, still recited in our churches today.

A hundred years later, another council was held, at Chalcedon, and the burning issue there was how Jesus could be both divine and human. I am not sure I understand many of the complex ideas debated at these councils, because most of the conclusions are based on principles of classic Greek metaphysics. Nevertheless, the theologians were wrestling with an essential faith issue: How does Jesus share a part of God?

Is there a more simple way to affirm how we see God in Jesus? Perhaps a phrase we use in my part of the country will help: "He's the spittin' image of his Daddy." Or we can say it more elegantly, using some ordinary theological words: "Jesus is like God, and God is like Jesus."

Do the people in your family resemble one another? Of course! There is a debate in our family about who my little granddaughter most resembles. She is a beautiful child with thick brown hair, sparkling brown eyes, and a smile that lights up a whole room. But who does Elizabeth look like—the Carys, her father's side of the family; or the Fellers, her mother's side? There is no doubt in her father's mind—she is a Cary through and through. But I think she looks like a Fellers, and I will always see a part of my heritage in her.

Just so with Jesus—he looks like God because we see God in him. However, the resemblance is not physical, it is relational. Jesus looks like God because their relationship is so intense, intimate, personal, and real that he acts like God. He loves, forgives, and accepts, just as God loves, forgives, and accepts. He is God with a face, because he does what we expect God to do.

We see the face of God in the mystery of life.

One of my favorite poets is G. A. Studdert-Kennedy. He was a clergyman in the Church of England, served as an Army chaplain in World War I, and returned to civilian life as the rector of a large, fashionable church in London. He was a powerful preacher, who also put some of the most profound truths of the Christian faith into beautiful, lyrical verse.

One of the most poignant stories he told is not in a poem, but about his first personal encounter with God, one night on the moors of Scotland. The sky was spangled with stars and waves were crashing on a nearby beach. Studdert-Kennedy felt a presence and wanted to call out, "Who's there?" but he was afraid. He said it was like some of the nights he later spent in the trenches during the war. He would sense someone was near and wanted to ask, "Who goes there?" but did not know whether the reply would be the sound of a bullet, a friendly voice, or silence.

Nevertheless, on the moor that night, he decided to risk it, so he shouted, "Who goes there?" He described what happened:

> "I made my cry . . . and I got my answer. I have sometimes doubted it, have never wholly understood it, but it remains. If I lost it I think I would lose my soul. I have been trying to say ever since one word—God. I stood that night in the presence of God."[1]

This is what it means to experience God in the mystery of life, and all of us can have such experiences if we are open to

25

them. They come in strange places—fishing early in the morning beside a sparkling fresh-water lake; watching the sun peep over the eastern horizon while out hunting; listening to beautiful music; holding a baby; slipping into the cool, quiet, shadows of an empty church.

Sometimes God seems very near to me while I am flying. Recently I had an opportunity to fly as a guest on a United States Air Force plane during a refueling mission. Only half a dozen people were on board, along with the crew. As I watched the aircraft go through a series of intricate maneuvers to refuel other planes, I thought about the poem "High Flight," written by John Gillespie Magee, Jr.:

> Oh, I have slipped the surly bonds of earth,
> And danced the skies on laughter-silvered wings;
> Sunward I've climbed and joined the tumbling mirth
> Of sun-split clouds—and done a hundred things
> You have not dreamed of—wheeled and soared and swung
> High in the sunlit silence. Hov'ring there,
> I've chased the shouting wind along and flung
> My eager craft through footless halls of air.
> Up, up the long, delicious, burning blue
> I've topped the wind-swept heights with easy grace,
> Where never lark, or even eagle, flew;
> And, while with silent, lifting mind I've trod
> The high untresspassed sanctity of space,
> Put out my hand, and touched the face of God.[2]

You don't need to be on an airplane to have a close, intimate, personal relationship with God—any place will do. If your heart is open, your mind receptive, and your spirit sensitive, you can reach out and touch the face of God where ever you are.

We see the face of God as events unfold.

Victor Hugo once observed that it had not been possible for Napoleon to win the battle of Waterloo. Why? "Not on account of Wellington, and not on account of Blucher, but on account of God. . . . Napoleon had been denounced and his fall decreed. Waterloo was not merely a battle; it was a trend of the universe."

When I read this comment, I thought about an account of the siege of Leningrad, now once again called St. Petersburg, during World War II. Harrison Evans Salisbury, in *900 Days: The Seige of Leningrad*, tells how Nazi armies stood poised on the outskirts of the city for almost three years. Some units even fought their way into the suburbs. Thousands of people died of starvation, and there were days when it seemed that the defenders could not hang on another hour. But finally the Germans, defeated at last by the bitter cold and the staunch defenders, retreated. There is a sense in which that defeat was inevitable, because God could not allow the forces of Hitler to win. His downfall was decreed; the moral forces of the universe demanded that he be vanquished.

What happens on the stage of history also happens to persons. A woman I knew was excited about the possibility of making a career change, but the opportunity fell through. She was disappointed and, for a long time, resented what had happened. Then another opportunity presented itself, and she eventually forgot about her past disappointment.

Years later, she realized that if the first opportunity had worked out, she would have missed some exciting experiences, as well as some wonderful people who had become cherished friends. There would have been an immense void in her life. She was convinced that God had been working in her life.

If you look back across events in your life, you may see the same process at work. God has an uncanny way of unfolding a purpose and plan through events that, to us, may seem to be random happenings.

We can see a divine presence at work in many events, if we look for it. It is not always apparent while those events are taking place—sometimes we have to wait years to realize it. Nevertheless, God is at work—sometimes in the forces of history, and always in the lives of people. We can see God's face if we are patient and wait for it to be revealed.

We see the face of God in people.

One of Leo Tolstoy's beautiful stories is about a promise Jesus made to a cobbler named Martin. In a dream, Jesus said to him, "Tomorrow I will visit you." So the next day, Martin got up early, swept his shop, prepared a delicious meal, and waited for the visit.

In the morning a hungry, exhausted child came to his shop, so Martin fed her and let her rest. At mid-day an old woman, pinched with cold, appeared, and Martin gave her a warm shawl. Late in the afternoon, a barefooted beggar came to the door, and Martin gave him a pair of shoes. But Jesus did not come, so that night Martin went to bed disappointed.

In a dream, Jesus appeared again, and Martin chided him: "Lord, why did you not visit me today?"

Jesus replied, "Martin, three times I visited you. First as a little child, then as an old woman, and finally as a beggar. When you have done it to one of the least of these, you have done it to me."

The moral of this parable is obvious—but how do we translate it into the world in which we live? Perhaps an incident from the life of Robert Kennedy will help to make it more contemporary. The senator, visiting South Africa, was asking in his abrupt, probing way about apartheid—a system of racial injustice in which persons who are black cannot vote, cannot own land except in a few places, earn wages 10 to 40 percent lower than their white counterparts, and black children receive only one-tenth of the amount the government spends to educate white children.

During a conversation with Kennedy, one person tried to justify the system by quoting selected verses from the Bible, but the senator interrupted with a question: "What if we go to heaven and we, all our lives, have treated the Negro as an inferior, and God is there, and we look up and he is not white? What then is our response? *Suppose God is black?*"[3] The response—silence.

A better answer would have been that God's face is black, white, yellow, brown, or any other skin pigment you can imagine. We Christians find God in strange places. Perhaps

God was in the face of a man who spent the night on the streets and slipped into a downtown business, looking for a place to clean up. Or was God in the face of a little boy who wanted to smile at a stranger but was afraid? Is God in the faces of young couples saying their marriage vows? Is God in the face of your husband, or wife, or child, or friend? Faith's answer: The face of God is anywhere people are, because the holy relates to the human in a personal relationship.

Now we have come full circle. The Sunday school teacher was right—nobody knows what God looks like. But the little girl was right, too. Somewhere, she had seen the face of God—she knew what God looked like. So look around—the face of God is anywhere you will take the time to find it.

Guess Who Came to the Sparrow's Funeral?

Discovering the Ways God Cares for Us

In his book *I Have Believed*, Earl Hunt affirms some of his beliefs about God and relates a fascinating incident that happened to him several years ago. He was visiting a church in Detroit, where one of his heroes, Dr. Merton Rice, had a long, distinguished pastorate. During his visit, Hunt recalled a story Dr. Rice's daughter had told about her father. Dr. Rice had been stricken by a heart attack, which later was to prove fatal, but he was still working on his sermons, especially the one he had hoped to preach when he returned to his pulpit. Though he never preached it, he shared some of what he wanted to say with his daughter, and she jotted it down. Here is what she wrote:

Oh! What a Heavenly Father We Have!

This is my story—about a little sparrow, shivering under a pile of damp leaves on a cold and dreary day. He was trying to keep warm and dry. He was the raggediest little sparrow in the whole world, dirty and spattered with mud. He couldn't find a single bite to eat, and the friends he had in the bird world had deserted him.

The little nest, once his house, had been demolished by wind and rain. He had no place to go, nor any energy left to build a new home. His tired little body gave up the feeble struggle to live, unnoticed by man or bird. No one cared or gave a thought to his death. But God, looking down from His throne, saw the small bird, alone and forgotten. He said, "I will go to the funeral of that sparrow. Not a sparrow falleth but that your Heavenly Father seeth it." What a Heavenly Father we have! He even attends the funerals of sparrows! God sees and hears and answers. Oh! what a Heavenly Father we have!

Hunt follows this winsome statement with an affirmation of his own about God's caring relationship with us: "There are surely more sophisticated and theological ways of saying it, but this simpler way conveys the truth, the glorious truth of the Christian message to all of us. God cares about you and me."[1]

When I read the paragraph Merton Rice sketched out, followed by Hunt's interpretation, I thought of several things.

One was an incident from my childhood. A friend of mine and I were playing one day when we found a dead bird. I have no idea why it died, but whatever the cause, I was repelled and fascinated by the tiny, lifeless brown and gray bird. As we looked at the dead sparrow, my friend and I decided to have a funeral for it. We did not know much about funerals, but both of us knew enough to get a small empty box, stuff it with tissue and cotton, pick some flowers from my mother's sweet-pea vines, and bury the sparrow. We even persuaded some girls to join us for the service. When the ceremonies were over, we marked the sparrow's grave with a stick and visited it several times during the following week.

I also remembered a vivid word picture I once read about an incident that could have occurred when Jesus was a little boy. The setting was the marketplace in Nazareth, near Joseph's carpenter shop. Jesus and his father were walking home for their mid-day meal. The youngster was looking at things for sale in the market—pottery, clothing, furniture, meat, and vegetables. The boy's eye caught something he had never seen before—a pile of tiny birds with their feathers rumpled, all dead. He did not understand why they were being sold, so he asked his father.

31

Joseph explained that some people were too poor to buy much food; sparrows were all they could afford. The little birds were cheap—two brass coins, each worth about a penny, would purchase four sparrows, and the dealer would give an extra one as a bonus. Joseph also told his son that even those sparrows, which cost next to nothing, were made by God, who loved them, and not one fell to the ground without God knowing what happened.[2]

That imaginary conversation helped me remember something Jesus said, "Are not two sparrows sold for a penny? Yet not one of them will fall to the ground apart from your Father" (Matt. 10:29). What a vivid way to affirm how much God cares for us. If God loves a sparrow enough to be concerned when its brief, frail life is over, how much more he must love us! This passage also reminds us that God expresses his care for us in a variety of ways, and I like to call the following ways the three "E's" of a trusting faith.

God enables us.

Once I was invited to give the invocation and benediction for the graduation ceremonies at a university attended primarily by African Americans. The commencement speaker was my good friend, Dr. E. Edward Jones, one of the great spiritual leaders of our time.

During his address, this gifted preacher talked about some of the struggles of his people in the context of his own experience. In the world in which Edward Jones and I grew up, there were two water fountains in department stores, one marked "White"; the other, "Colored." In most public places there were three restrooms: "Men," "Women," and "Colored." Schools were separate, but rarely equal. Black people sat in the back of the bus, while white people sat in the front. Ours was a closed, segregated society—black people were told that they could go only so far.

Then God began to enable all of us. The process started on December 1, 1955, in Montgomery, Alabama, when a black woman, Rosa Parks, was on her way home from work, riding a crowded bus. A white person got on, and Mrs. Parks was expected to move to the back and stand—but her feet hurt, and she refused to budge.

By coincidence—or was it by design—there was a young preacher in Montgomery named Martin Luther King, Jr.—and the rest is history. Mrs. Parks sparked a revolution that changed attitudes in this country. God enabled her to protest the blight of racial segregation in a sensible, practical, sympathetic fashion. God enabled a preacher with a brilliant mind and unusual eloquence to arouse the conscience of a nation. And God continues to enable people to believe that black and white together can overcome prejudice and alienation to build a fairer and better world.

"Oh! What a Heavenly Father we have!" Not a sparrow falls without God knowing about it, and not a person's feet hurt without God being aware of it.

God empowers us.

There are many unanswered questions about how God gives us the power to do things that seem impossible. Does God stir up a latent energy inside us of which we are not aware? Does God touch us with a special measure of God's own strength? Does God permit us to take advantage of the untapped resources of the universe without our realizing it? Or is God's gift of power a combination of all these possibilities, and more? I do not know, but I am convinced the power is there, and it is ours for the asking, if we are brave enough to take advantage of it.

Perhaps you and I are like a young bear who was trying to learn to walk. He asked his mother, "Shall I move my right paw first, or my left? Or shall I move my front two paws, and then my two back paws? Or the ones on the right, and then the ones on the left? Should I try to move all my paws at one time?" When you think about it, walking can be complicated—but the mother bear wisely told her son, "Stop thinking about it—just walk!" Perhaps you and I should not spend a lot of time thinking about how we receive God's empowering gifts—we should just use them.

When I have trusted God to see me through difficult

situations, I have always been provided with the resources I needed. While I was serving as president of a small college in east Texas, several friends whose worship services were televised invited me to preach from their pulpits. But I always managed to find a tactful excuse to refuse their invitations, pleading a conflict in schedule or a previous commitment. I was afraid to preach on TV.

One day a friend invited me to preach for him because he was to be out of his pulpit. I tried to turn down the invitation, but my friend would not be put off. I had no alternative but to confess that I was petrified at the prospect of preaching in front of television cameras.

He was sympathetic—"John," he said, "I was apprehensive the first time I preached on TV, but think about the opportunity you will have. Your message will be heard by more people than many preachers preach to in a lifetime." How do you refuse such an invitation? I had no choice but to accept.

The Saturday night before I was scheduled to preach, I tossed and turned for hours. As I drove to the church, my stomach churned, and I was a bundle of nerves. But when I walked into the sanctuary and started to sing the first hymn, a strange assurance flooded my entire being. When I stood up to preach, I felt a power I had never felt before in the pulpit. Since that day, I have never been afraid to preach on television.

How did God give me the power to work through my anxiety? I do not know—but God did give it, and the results are what finally count.

Another example of God's hidden power at work is recounted by Norman Cousins in his *Anatomy of an Illness*. After a trip to Russia, that distinguished editor and author was stricken by a mysterious malady that baffled his doctors. Nodules appeared all over his body; he could barely move, and at one point his jaws almost locked. His doctors were pessimistic about his chances for survival.

Since he was getting no better, Cousins checked himself out of the hospital, rented a hotel room, and started watching old Marx Brothers movies and replays of the popular television program from the fifties, "Candid Camera." His recovery was slow and painful, but in a few months he was back at his desk as the editor of *Saturday Review*. Discussing his miraculous recovery, Cousins said, "I have learned never to underestimate the capacity of the human mind and body to regenerate—even when its prospects seem most wretched" (p. 48).

Where did the regenerative power to heal Cousins' diseased body come from? I am convinced it was a gift from God. This power is available to all of us. God offers it to each of us and wants us to take advantage of it. It does more than heal our bodies—it resolves our fears, relieves our anxieties, and restores our souls. The power is ours for the asking.

God encircles us.

When I was growing up, some friends of my parents had a picture hanging in their living room that fascinated me each time I saw it. Though I have no idea who painted it or its title, I can see it on the canvas of my imagination as vividly as if it were hanging in my own home today.

The picture was of two children, a boy and girl, crossing a raging river on an old-fashioned suspension bridge. The bridge was flimsy and looked as if it could collapse at any moment. Standing on one side of the bridge was a guardian angel, invisible to the children, but keeping watch over them.

When I looked at that picture as a child—and when I think of it now—I believe the angel was a "God symbol" for me. I saw this messenger from heaven as one who represented a loving, gracious Heavenly Father, watching over the children, encircling them with love and care. I am convinced that God watches over us with this kind of protective love, and if we were more aware of it, much of our worry, fear, and anxiety would vanish.

Elizabeth Chaney confirms this conviction in a whimsical little poem, "Overheard in an Orchard," which describes a dialogue between a robin and a sparrow:

> Said the Robin to the Sparrow:
> "I should really like to know

Why these anxious human beings
Rush about and worry so."

Said the Sparrow to the Robin:
"Friend, I think that it must be
That they have no heavenly Father
Such as cares for you and me."

Knowing that we have a Heavenly Father who cares about sparrows tells us something about our own relationship with God.

During the View Nam war, a young naval airman named Michael Schafernocker was killed in a soiree over Cambodia. Just before he went on his last mission, he wrote a poem that he called "Look, God." Later his mother found it in Michael's personal affects when they were shipped home. The verses are a touching explanation of the way we discover God's loving care when we need it most.

Look, God, I have never spoken to you,
But now I want to say "How do you do."
You see, God, they told me you didn't exist.
And like a fool I believed all this.

Last night from a shell hole I saw your starry sky.
I figured right then they had told me a lie.
Had I taken time to see things you made,
I'd have known they weren't calling a spade a spade.

I wonder, God, if you'd take my hand.
Somehow, I feel you will understand.
Funny, I had to come to this hellish place
Before I had time to see your face.

Well, I guess there isn't much more to say,
But I'm sure glad, God, I met you today.
I guess the zero hour will soon be here,
But I'm not afraid since I know you're near.

The signal—well, God, I'll have to go.
I like you lots and I want you to know.
Look, now, this will be a horrible fight
Who knows, I may come to your house tonight.

Though I wasn't friendly to you before,
I wonder, God, if you'd wait at the door.
Look, I'm crying. Me, shedding tears!
I wish I'd known you these many years.

Well, I have to go now, God, good-bye;
Strange, since I've met you I'm not afraid to die.[3]

"Oh! What a Heavenly Father we have!" God is with us on every step of life's journey, even to the doorway of eternity.

Wisdom from
a Sandbox

Getting Back
to Basics

Robert Fulghum begins his intriguing book *All I Really Need to Know I Learned in Kindergarten* in this way:

ALL I REALLY NEED TO KNOW about how to live and what to do and how to be I learned in kindergarten. Wisdom was not at the top of the graduate-school mountain, but there in the sandpile at Sunday School. These are the things I learned:

Share everything.

Play fair.

Don't hit people.

Put things back where you found them.

Clean up your own mess.

Don't take things that aren't yours.

Say you're sorry when you hurt somebody.

Wash your hands before you eat.

Flush.

Warm cookies and cold milk are good for you.

Live a balanced life—learn some and think some and draw and paint and sing and dance and play and work every day some.

Take a nap every afternoon.

When you go out into the world, watch out for traffic, hold hands, and stick together.

Be aware of wonder. Remember the little seed in the

Styrofoam cup: The roots go down and the plant goes up and nobody really knows how or why, but we are all like that.

Goldfish and hamsters and white mice and even the little seed in the Styrofoam cup—they all die. So do we.

And then remember the Dick-and-Jane books and the first word you learned—the biggest word of all—LOOK.

Everything you need to know is in there somewhere. The Golden Rule and love and basic sanitation. Ecology and politics and equality and sane living.

Take any one of those items and extrapolate it into sophisticated adult terms and apply it to your family life or your work or your government or your world and it holds true and clear and firm. Think what a better world it would be if we all—the whole world—had cookies and milk about three o'clock every afternoon and then lay down with our blankies for a nap. Or if all governments had as a basic policy to always put things back where they found them and to clean up their own mess.

And it is still true, no matter how old you are—when you go out into the world, it is best to hold hands and stick together.[1]

When I read Mr. Fulghum's comments, I was enchanted. He awakened dormant memories of my first days in school, and I knew he had stumbled upon a profound truth about life—in a sandbox, there is wisdom that we learn nowhere else.

A hint of this idea is found in one of the letters that was circulated in the early church and eventually incorporated into the New Testament. We do not know who wrote the letter, but it is part of a triology credited to the pen of John. The first letter of John may not have been a letter at all—it has no salutation or conclusion—so it may have been a sermon that was passed from one congregation to another. Whatever the circumstances of its writing, a tenderness underlays the entire document. Time and again, the writer addresses the readers as "little children," almost as if they were Christians in the kindergarten phase of their faith experience; there is a caress in many of those words.

At times, each of us, regardless of how wise we may be or how mature we are, need to deal with life from a kindergarten perspective. This is not an invitation to be childish; it is a suggestion to help establish a value system that will determine what is ultimately important. Everyone needs such a system, so think about the following four of Robert Fulghum's suggestions and relate them to the way you deal with reality.

Wake up to wonder.

Do you ever wish you could get as excited about things as you did when you where a child? I do. Sometimes I wish that a growing flower, a holiday, a trip to the beach, or a shopping expedition could make me stand on the tiptoe of expectation, as it did almost fifty years ago.

To be honest, I suspect that all these things and many more could be exciting if I took time to cultivate the art of wonder. Instead, I allow myself to become overcommitted, overprogrammed, and overscheduled. I rush through life day after day, without realizing I am losing some of the beauty and enchantment around me.

A vital faith must begin with a sense of wonder. In *Fresh Every Morning*, the late Gerald Kennedy observed, "The mood of true religion is one of wonder and awe. . . . Standing before the majesty of God and seeing all the wonder of His involvment in human life, man breaks into poetry if he is able, but at the very least he stands in silence" (p. 31).

Kennedy also pointed out that much of the spiritual poverty of our time can be traced to a loss of reverence. We lack a capacity for wonder, but deep within ourselves we yearn for something that touches the deepest mystery of things.

One of the most beautiful cities in the world is Vienna, where the magnificent St. Stephen's Cathedral stands in the heart of the city. Built in the thirteenth century, the cathedral was almost destroyed during World War II. It was first bombed and then caught in the crossfire of the two opposing armies as they fought for posession for the city.

When the war was over Vienna was prostrate. There was barely enough food to feed the people, the economy was in a shambles, and thousands of homes had been destroyed. But one of the first things the people of Vienna did was to begin the rebuilding of their beloved cathedral. They hauled rubble when they hardly had enough to eat. They lavished gifts upon the church when the country was almost bankrupt. They overcame overwhelming obstacles to complete the reconstruction. Can you guess why? Because in those bleak, dreary years of defeat, the people of the city needed a sense of wonder to keep them in touch with the eternal.

God will give us this sense of wonder if we are sensitive enough to accept it. One of the most profound thinkers of our time was Rabbi Abraham Joshua Heschel. A few years before his death in 1972, he suffered an almost fatal heart attack from which he never fully recovered. When a friend went to visit, he found Heschel very weak, but the rabbi wanted to talk about what had happened.

"Sam," he said, "when I regained consciousness, my first feeling was not despair or anger. I felt only gratitude to God for every moment I had lived. I was ready to depart. 'Take me, O Lord,' I thought. 'I have seen so many miracles in my lifetime.' " Almost exhausted, Heschel paused and continued, "That is what I meant when I wrote . . . 'I did not ask for success, I asked for wonder. And You gave it to me.' "[2]

God gives us wonder every day—sometimes in great events, sometimes in small ones. Wonder comes when a human being walks on the moon or when a rose blooms. Wonder echos in great music or lingers with a kiss. Sometimes wonder is in laughter; at other times, it touches us with tears. Wonder is even in bean sprouts, growing in a plastic cup, if we will only watch for it and enjoy it.

Take time to look.

When I was a youngster about eleven or twelve years old, my family took a trip to Hot Springs, Arkansas. This was the first automobile trip I remember because gasoline was rationed for several years, so my folks could not travel for pleasure. I was so excited about going to Hot Springs, I could hardly wait to get there. To pass the time in the back seat of the car, I read comic books. My parents suggested I put the books away and look at the scenery—but after a few minutes I would pick up another comic book and start reading again.

Eventually we arrived in Hot Springs, and I was the most disappointed youngster you can imagine because it was not what I expected. There were no springs erupting out of the ground, nor did I see any streams gushing through the streets. Hot Springs looked like any other other city; the only difference was the large number of hotels scattered around town.

In my disappointment, I learned a lesson—getting to a place can be as much fun as arriving there. This idea is expressed in a phrase we often hear: "Life is not so much a destination as a journey." Unfortunately, many of us do not take time to look around as we make our life journey. We rush headlong, trying to get from one destination to another, so we miss a lot of interesting experiences along the way.

One evening I happened to watch a British public television program about a young man who was executed in Mississippi. He had been sentenced to die in the gas chamber for the killing of a police officer several years before. The program recorded the events leading up to his execution— the last minute appeals, hopes for clemency, and preparations inside the prison.

Two things during the program touched me and I have never forgotten them. The first incident occurred when a reporter asked the condemned man what he had missed most during the seven years he had lived on death row. Can you imagine his answer? He missed being able to see the moon and the stars. The other thing I shall always remember was the menu of the prisoner's last meal, which included shrimp. He had never eaten shrimp until the evening he was scheduled to die.

I thought to myself, how often have you gone out at night and never bothered to look up at the moon? How often do you notice the stars? I also recalled that a couple of evenings before, I had a delicious dinner of shrimp and crab, but I never gave the meal a second thought after my hunger was satisified.

Savor life while you experience it. Don't wait until it is too late, and then look back at things you did not take time to enjoy, regretting what you missed.

Clean up your own mess.

My parents used to tell me something I have tried to instill in my own children: "If you pick up your own things, it's easy to keep the house clean." Kindergarten teachers also attempt to teach this principle to their students; they make sure they leave their classrooms neat and tidy at the end of each day. If they did not do this, the room would not be fit to live in by the end of the week. There is a valuable lesson in learning how to clean up after yourself.

I learned this lesson as a teenager when I had a paper route. One afternoon after I had finished delivering my papers, I met a friend. As we bicycled home, we noticed that garbage had been collected that day, and all the empty cans were sitting on the curb. At that time, garbage cans were made out of galvanized tin, so when my friend and I started to kick them over, the entire street sounded like a battle zone. We kicked cans for several blocks, he on one side and I on the other.

Then the unexpected happened. A friend of my father drove by and saw what was happening. He stopped his car, and before I could open my mouth, he said, "Johnny, I want you to pick up every garbage can you and your friend have knocked over. I'm going to follow you, and unless these cans are put back in place, I'm going to call your father." There was nothing to do but pick up the mess I had made.

I have had to pick up a lot of messes I have made during the years that followed—sometimes with an apology, admitting I was wrong; picking up the pieces of a failure; or trying to heal a relationship I have fractured. Learning how to clean up your own mess is a valuable lesson. We begin to learn it while we are playing in the sandbox, but it is a lesson we need to carry with us all our lives.

Join hands to build a better world.

Some time ago, a group of Russians came to the television studios at the church where I was pastor, to do a special program. Though the first stirrings of democracy were taking place in what was then the Soviet Union, there was much skepticism in the West about how genuine the reforms were. And that was the first time I had ever been involved in a personal encounter with citizens of the USSR.

The visit proved to be delightful; I found Russians much like Americans—warm, friendly, and eager to know people. They were scheduled to spend the morning becoming familiar with the TV facilities, then we were to have lunch.

When it was time to sit down, I was in a quandry. I am accustomed to saying grace before meals, but I suspected that most of our guests were not believers. Should I pray—or not? A wiser friend, also a minister, covered my moment of hesitation.

He said, "John, why don't we all join hands while you ask the blessing?" The entire group—several Americans and about a dozen Russians—clasped hands and I prayed. When I said "Amen," I squeezed the hands of the people standing next to me, and they squeezed mine. During the prayer, the barriers of politics and philosophy came tumbling down. By holding hands, we all became real human beings to one another.

I have thought of this episode many times, and I'm now convinced that as long as people can hold hands, they can work together to build a better world. The problem is, we often forget to reach out for one another. But what a difference it makes when we remember!

Early in my ministry I was invited by a friend to preach at Youth Week. It was during a time when racial tensions were running high in our country and the first voices of dissent were being raised about our involvment in Viet Nam. When my colleague extended the invitation, he made an unusual request—he asked me to tell this story:

A little girl, about four years old, lived at the edge of the desert in California. One afternoon when she went out to play, she wandered out of her yard, and before anyone knew what had happened she was lost. When the child's mother could not find her, she called for help, and within minutes a search team was mobilized. Law enforcement officers came from nearby towns, and helicopters flew over the area, all trying to locate the little girl. But when the sun began to set, the chances of finding her diminished by the minute.

At dusk, one of the searchers had a brilliant idea—why not join hands and comb every inch of the area near the child's home? So all the members of the search party held hands and walked in a straight line. Within an hour, they found the little girl crouched in a gulley about a mile from her home, cold and frightened but safe and unharmed.

When the child was taken back to her mother, the woman tried to express her thanks, but all she could say was, "Thank God, you joined hands soon enough!"

"When you go out into the world, it's best to hold hands and stick together." That is sandbox wisdom—one of those simple things we learned in kindergarten. But a sandbox may be the place where God starts teaching us how to help redeem the world.

Whistle While You Work

Finding Meaning in Your Job

Have you ever taken a few minutes to analyze how you spend your time? If you are a typical American, you sleep about seven hours out of twenty-four. You take roughly an hour and a half to eat three meals, and you probably use a couple of hours each day doing such mundane things as brushing your teeth, carrying out the trash, driving from one place to another, or stopping at the grocery to pick up a few items. But most of your time is spent at your job. The average person in our country works between eight and ten hours, five or six days each week. This means you spend 60 percent of your waking hours in the workplace, and you will work about 80,000 hours during your lifetime.

It is amazing how much time we spend doing our jobs, but how little time exploring the spiritual dimensions of our work. Many people, either consciously or subsconsciously, feel work is a curse.

Several years ago, a large eastern newspaper carried an advertisement:

WANTED: A man to live alone on an island in an inland lake. Transportation, food, cabin, and boat furnished. No work and no pay. Address: Mr. Sunshine, Tribune Bldg., New York, N.Y.

"Mr. Sunshine" was a fictitious character, but the ad was real. A wealthy New Yorker wanted someone to keep watch at an island where seagulls from Manhatten flew to hatch their young. More than 1,600 persons applied for this position, which promised only peace and quiet, at a remote, lonely place where they could get away from the pressure of their jobs.[1]

There is, however, a more positive side to work; it is an essential ingredient which gives life meaning. When I was a youngster and started taking music lessons, one of the first songs I learned was "Whistle While You Work," from Walt Disney's movie *Snow White and the Seven Dwarfs.* The person who wrote that song discovered an important secret about living an exciting life. When we feel happy and fulfilled in our work, we have a sense of dignity and purpose. When we lose this sense of fulfillment, we become mentally, spiritually, and emotionally stale.

During World War II, a group imprisoned at a Nazi concentration camp in Hungary converted waste products into synthetic alcohol to be used as a fuel additive. One day the Allies bombed the camp and almost destroyed the building where the alcohol was manufactured. The next morning the guards decided to punish the inmates. They forced them to take all the rubble from the air-raid and arrange it at one end of a field. When the prisoners finished this task, the guards ordered them to carry it back to the other end. This went on, back and forth, for several weeks until the prisoners began to break under the strain. Some tried to escape and were killed. Others electrocuted themselves by jumping on the high-voltage fence that surrounded the camp. A few lost their minds because the work made no sense—their lives had no meaning.[2]

Our Christian faith gives a fascinating insight into the dignity of work in a cryptic comment Jesus made after he healed a lame man on the sabbath. When he was criticized for violating sabbath law, the Master reminded his critics, "My Father is still working, and I also am working" (John 5:17). Jesus was subtly saying that his work and God's work were the same. He also implied something else in this simple,

47

direct statement—one of the common denominators between the divine and the human is work. God is always at work, creating and sustaining life, while you and I work to give life meaning. To discover this meaning, there are some basic principles each of us should remember about our work.

A job is more than a task.

There is a beautiful story about some men who were building the magnificent cathedral which stands on the banks of the Rhine River in Colonge, Germany. A tourist, wandering through the church and marveling at its exquisite architecture, stepped over to a carpenter and asked what he was doing. Without even looking up, the carpenter brusquely replied, "I am sawing wood."

A few minutes later, the tourist encountered a glass worker and asked the same question. This time the worker was a bit more courteous: "I am making some of the stained glass for the windows that will be placed in this church."

The tourist noticed a stone mason at work and asked the question again. The mason stopped, stood up to his full height, and replied, "Sir, I am building a cathedral!" This man knew that his work would bless each person who worshiped in the cathedral for centuries to come. He was aware that his work had meaning beyond a paycheck. It was his way of getting people in touch with God.

To find meaning in our jobs, you and I need to make a distinction between just doing something to earn a living and doing something that has meaning. We have many tasks to complete every day, but our jobs are more than the sum total of these chores. A task can be accomplished by meeting a specific objective—creative work is an opportunity to touch the lives of others, to make them richer and better.

I discovered this without realizing it when I was a youngster, working at my first job. Like a lot of boys when I was growing up, I had a paper route. I put two canvas bags on the back of my bicycle, folded newspapers, bound them with twine, and threw them on the porches of my customers. For months, I assumed that my job was to deliver the newspapers by six o'clock in the evening, get home and be ready for supper a few minutes later.

One evening after I had finished throwing my papers, my family and I sat down to eat. The telephone rang; it was one of my customers, complaining she had not received her paper. I apologized and explained that someone probably picked it up before she had gone out to get it. This excuse did not placate my irate customer, so I promised I would not charge her for that days paper—and that did not satisfy her either.

"Johnny," she said, "I want my paper tonight! If I don't get it, how will I know what happened today?" I did not dare suggest that she listen to the news on the radio; instead, I told her that as soon as we were through with supper, my dad would drive me over to bring another paper.

I learned a valuable lesson from that episode. A job is more than just "doing something" or making a living—it is part of our relationship with the people around us. When you and I discover this secret about our work, we are able to focus on more than a specific task or a day's schedule. We begin to catch a glimpse of how our job fits into a grander scheme of things. We relate our work to God's purpose for Creation, and we see our job as an opportunity to enrich and enlarge quality of life for the entire human family.

Work can be more than drudgery.

A certain amount of drudgery is involved in every profession, regardless of how exciting it may appear to outsiders. None of us can escape the fact that some of our work will be tiresome and exhausting, as well as exciting and worthwhile. Our attitudes determine whether a job is creative work or grinding toil.

Two women were employed to clean a large office building. Each day, after everyone had gone home, they would come to the building, sweep the floors, dust the desks, and empty wastebaskets. One of them hated her job, so one evening she blurted out her resentment: "All I do is work like a slave!" Her companion answered, "But dearie, you could work like a queen."

Each of us can choose how we work—with dignity, poise, and grace, or with resentment, bitterness, and anger. Which we choose determines what our job means to us; whether it is a pathway to fulfillment or a constant round of toil.

When Winston Churchill finished his epic series, *A History of the English-speaking Peoples,* a literary critic for a London newspaper asked him how he was able to write such splendid books and, at the same time, maintain a high profile in public life as a member of Parliment and world leader, speaking out on a variety of current issues. Mr. Churchill explained that each day he assigned himself a certain number of pages to complete, and he did not stop until he reached the mark he had set for himself. He described his method in graphic terms by declaring that he took himself "by the seat of the pants" and wrote until that day's section was done.

This routine must have been exhausting for such a busy man. You can visit his study at Chartwell, his country home, and see the waist-high desk where he stood and the area in which he paced up and down, dictating to a relay of secretaries. Fortunately, Winston Churchill could see beyond the daily grind, the grueling routine, and the tremendous amount of energy he expended while writing. He produced a great piece of literature and a fascinating study of human events because he could distinguish between exciting work and unimaginative toil.

Are you bored with your job, worn out every morning before you get started, tired before the day has begun? Perhaps you should learn the difference between work and drudgery, because the perspective from which you look at your job goes a long way toward determining the way you react to it.

Satisfaction is more than earning a salary.

Psychologists who have studied our motivation to work contend that most of us work for two reasons. One is to provide the material needs of those we love; the other is to find a sense of accomplishment in knowing we are doing something worthwhile.

During one of the periodic layoffs in the automotive industry, several men found themselves idle for the first time in years. Most had no financial problems, since they had unemployment compensation and a union fund from which to draw. They enjoyed the break in the routine for a while—it was like an extended vacation.

Before long, however, time began to hang heavy on the hands of some of them. A few discovered they had no reason to get up in the morning. There was nothing to do; their whole lives seemed out of focus. Finally, one laid-off worker realized that he needed something to do—any kind of job—so he decided to paint his house. This decision saved his sanity until he was called back to his job at the automotive plant. As he painted, this man discovered a basic secret about work: The satisfaction of doing a job is worth more than being paid for it.

One of the industrial giants of the twentieth century was Henry Ford. He had an uncanny knack of finding out what made a machine work and how its energy could be harnessed to help people. At the beginning of his career he tinkered with automobiles, trying to discover how they could be converted from toys for the rich into a cheap, efficient means of transportation for the masses. One of his biographers, Robert Lacy, says that Ford wanted to "share the joy of machines with the world."

In 1907, Ford began to dream about a car that would soon transform the American way of life. It was called the Model T, and eventually became the most popular car ever produced in this country. Before he began production, Ford told some friends and prospective shareholders:

> I will build a motor car for the great multitude. It will be large enough for the family, but small enough for the individual to run and care for. It will be constructed of the best materials, by the best men to be hired, after the simplest designs that modern engineering can devise. But it will be so low in price that no man making a good salary will be unable to own one—and enjoy with his family the blessing of hours of pleasure in God's great open spaces.[3]

Though Henry Ford made many mistakes during his long career as an industrialist, he discovered the secret of finding satisfaction in work. We should labor with our hands, minds, and bodies to make the world a better place in which to live. The ultimate reward for doing a job is more than money.

This is the great secret of being able to "whistle while you work." The satisfaction you crave at your job is not hidden in your paycheck. You cannot grasp it by taking two steps at a time up the corporate ladder, getting more perks, or receiving larger stock options. The real joy of work is knowing that while you work, God is also working, and there is something holy in what both of you are doing!

If at First
You Don't Succeed

Learning to Cope
with Failure

When I was about seven or eight years old, we visited my uncle and aunt who lived on a farm in central Texas. Our arrival coincided with cotton-picking time, and since I was from the city, I was fascinated with cotton growing in the fields. The bushes were bronzed by the sun, acres of farmland looked as if a blizzard had blown in the night before, and the cotton itself was bursting in the pod.

My uncle brought in people to help with the picking. My cousins went to the fields to lend a hand, so I pleaded with my parents to let me pick cotton, and they finally agreed. My uncle found a small cotton sack, a sweat band, and a straw hat. He promised to pay me for every pound of cotton I picked, so I fell asleep that night with visions of sacks overflowing with cotton and my pockets stuffed with dollar bills.

The next morning, when the farm bell rang at 5:30 A.M., I tumbled out of bed, dressed as quickly as possible, and went downstairs to eat breakfast. A half-hour later, I got into my uncle's truck with my cousins and the other workers, and we drove to the fields. When we arrived, my uncle took me in tow and showed me how to extract the little ball of cotton from the pod in which it grew. The process looked easy, so I started to work.

I was a slow picker, but for a while everything went well. Then my cousins got ahead of me, my back started to ache, and the sun began to beat down on my head. Before long I found myself alone, hot, aching, and exhausted, with almost no cotton in my sack. I was frustrated—and then I stepped into a bed of fire ants. Before I knew what was happening, I was stung from head to toe.

About that time my uncle drove by and found a little boy crying, frantically trying to get rid of the ants that were stinging him, with less than a pound of cotton in his sack. He brushed me off, lifted me into this truck, and we went back to the house, where my aunt scolded everybody for letting me go to the fields in the first place.

That evening when my cousins came to the house, they started asking some embarrassing questions—wanting to know how much cotton I had picked and how much money I had made. I was humiliated. For the first time in my life, I was experiencing total, unmitigated failure.

Everyone has had such an experience and each of us can remember the first time we failed. It is embarrassing, and it makes an indelible impression that none of us can forget. Even Jesus experienced failure, and two such incidents are recorded in the Gospel according to Matthew.

One occurred early in Jesus' ministry, in the area where he grew up. His fame had spread across northern Galilee because he was a charismatic teacher and gifted healer. But the people in his hometown did not take him seriously.

Finally Jesus told them, "Prophets are not without honor except in their own country and in their own house." The writer adds a poignant footnote: "And he did not do many deeds of power there, because of their unbelief" (Matt. 13:57-58).

The second example of failure in the ministry of Jesus occurred during the last climatic week of his life. He went to Jerusalem, hoping to take a final decisive step to inaugurate the kingdom about which he preached; instead, he was caught up in the religious and political tensions of the city. One day, in despair, he must have walked out to one of the

54

hills that surround Jerusalem, looked across the rooftops of the town with a heavy heart, and said:

> "Jerusalem, Jerusalem, the city that kills the prophets and stones those that are sent to it! How often have I desired to gather your children together as a hen gathers her brood under her wings, and you were not willing!" (Matt. 23:37).

At that moment Jesus realized that his ministry to the city had failed. No doubt he suspected he would have a rendezvous with a cross before the week was out.

Since failure is so much a part of living, you and I must learn to cope with it. Leo Tolstoy, in his autobiography *Confessions*, says there are four ways to deal with failure. One is to become frightened and get drunk. Another is to lapse into despair and take your own life. The third is to resent failure and let it destroy you. The fourth is to accept it and deal with it creatively.

An old proverb provides a clue about how to use our faith and come to grips with our failures: "If at first you don't succeed, try, try again." This is sound advice, but before we try again, we should understand some crucial things about the dynamics of failure and how to live beyond it.

Everybody fails, so no one is exempt from its curse.

Even people who appear to be highly successful must admit there are goals they cannot achieve, things they cannot do, circumstances they cannot control. Though I was a reasonably good student in high school, I had an encounter with failure in the tenth grade. The college I planned to attend required entering freshmen to have at least two credits in algebra. So I enrolled in Algebra, and from the first day in class, I was lost in a maze of confusion. I never understood how "x" could equal "y" or how letters of the alphabet could have numerical values, so I failed the course. To get my algebra credit, I enrolled in summer school and managed to pass because I went to class every day. But that was only one credit, and I needed two! The next fall I signed up for a second unit of algebra and failed again! I went to summer school a second time and finally managed to pass Albegra II. I still consider myself a math drop-out; I do not understand any more about algebra today than I did thirty-five years ago.

I recently discovered I am in elite company. Both Albert Einstein and Werner von Braun flunked math courses. Enrico Caruso, one of the greatest tenors of all time, missed his high notes so often, his voice coach told him to forget about a career in music. One of Thomas Edison's teachers called him a dunce, and after he was a successful inventor, he conducted 14,000 experiments before he perfected the electric light. People who fail are in good company, because the most successful of us fail in one venture or another. Failure is an inevitable part of the human experience.

Failures are not always our fault.

We sometimes fail because of circumstances beyond our control. This kind of failure happened to me in another classroom situation. In my seventh-grade science class, each student was assigned a project in which to make a practical application of some of the theories we were learning. I chose to build a simple motor made of large nails mounted on a block of wood. The process looked simple, so I drove several nails into the wood, taped four of them together to create an armature, and wired them to a dry-cell battery which made the armature turn.

I built my motor at home, tested it several times, and during each test it ran perfectly. The day our projects were due, I wrapped my motor carefully, packed it in a shoe box, and took it to school. When it was time for my classroom demonstration, the armature would not turn. It sat frozen and still; no amount of tinkering would make the motor work. Fortunately, my science teacher suspected I had damaged the armature bringing it to class, so she let me call my father, who came and repaired it. Though the motor eventually worked as it was supposed to, my demonstration was a failure.

The same phenomena happen in many areas of life; we fail because of an unfortunate collision of events and circumstances beyond our control.

One evening while playing a board game, I was asked to name my favorite movie. In an instant, I knew which one I would pick—*Dr. Zhivago.* Later, I reflected that one of the themes in the movie is about failure. Zhivago dies on a Moscow steetcar, his "Laura" poems known only to a few. He never fit into the new society that emerged when his safe, comfortable world fell apart. His creativity was stifled by a totalitarian state. Nor did he seriously practice medicine, the profession for which he was trained. But Zhivago's failures were not his fault; he was a victim of the time and place where he lived and worked.

So if our failures are not always our fault, how should we react to them?

No failure is final unless we want it to be.

In 1987, Charles E. "Buddy" Roemer III was elected governor of Louisiana. His inauguration was an exciting event.

But Governor Roemer's first brush with politics had not been so successful. In 1978, he lost his bid for Congress, but he refused to let that failure become final. Instead, he transformed his defeat into a learning experience. Two years later he ran for the same Congressional seat and was elected. He launched his successful bid for governor after serving several terms in the House of Representatives.

Recently, the governor had another brush with failure. Caught in a three-way race as he made a bid for reelection, he lost. But I suspect we have not heard the last of him.

Apparent failure is a familiar tradition in American politics. In 1831, there was a man who failed in business; in 1836, he had a nervous breakdown; in 1838 he was defeated in the voting for Speaker of the House in his state legislature. In 1848, he lost the Congressional seat to which he had been elected two years before, and his appointment as a federal land commissioner was rejected. The next year, he lost a bid for the United State Senate. In 1856 he lost his party's nomination for Vice President, and two years later he was defeated in another Senate race. But in 1860, Abraham Lincoln was elected President of the United States, and the rest, as they say, is history.

What do you think motivated Lincoln to keep on trying when one defeat followed another? He must have believed his failures were not final unless he wanted them to be.

Weigh the dynamics of success and failure in your life. Haven't you learned as much from your failures as from your successes? I have. As I look back across my life—to a cotton field, a science project, an algebra class, and all the other places where I missed the mark or fell short of a goal—I know that during those failures, I was growing, learning, and maturing.

I am sure I shall fail again, so for me failure is not so much a curse as an opportunity. If used creatively, failure can become a stepping stone to personal growth.

A few lines of poetry by an unknown author help me to deal with my failures, and I believe they can help you to put your failures into perspective, so you can grow beyond them:

> Weep not for precious chances passed away,
> Wait not for golden ages on the wane:
> Each night I burn the records of that day,
> At sunrise every soul is born again.

Defeating the
Green-eyed Monster

Resolving Our
Feelings of Jealousy

I once heard a fascinating story about crabs. A young man was walking on a beach when he encountered an older man getting ready to catch crabs. Since he had never seen anyone catch crabs, the young man was fascinated by the process. The crabber tied a chicken neck on a string, dropped it into the water, and tied the other end securely to the pier. He set up a dozen strings in this manner, and an hour or so later started checking them. Sure enough, there were crabs on several of the strings, so the man scooped them up with a net and threw them into a large bucket.

The young fellow watched this routine for a while. It wasn't long until the bucket was half full and claws and crab legs began to appear at the top. So he became alarmed and said to the crabber, "Mister, you better put a top on your bucket or all your crabs are going to escape!" The older, wiser man replied, "Not a chance, sonny. Every time one of them gets to the top, the others will pull him down!"

This story about crabs is an exquisite parable about human nature, because each of us has something of a crab in us. As soon as people become too successful, achieve too much, or accumulate too many things, you and I try to pull them down. This dynamic of human nature is called jealousy. None of us is exempt from it—even the disciples of Jesus had to contend with this personality flaw, often called the green-eyed monster.

On one occasion, perhaps just a few weeks before Jesus went to the cross, two of his disciples, James and John, asked him for a special favor. They believed he would establish his kingdom on earth in the near future. Perhaps its consummation was only weeks or months away, so they wanted special places of honor when the kingdom dawned. One wanted to sit at Jesus' right hand, the other at his left. When the other disciples heard what James and John had done, they were furious (cf. Mark 10:35-45).

This unfortunate incident could have destroyed the tight little band of intimate followers, but in his ingenious way, Jesus dealt with the ambition of James and John, as well as the jealousy of their colleagues. First he asked the brothers if they were prepared to share his suffering; then he explained that only God could assign places of honor in the kingdom; and finally, he reminded them that whoever would be great in his scheme of things must be the servant of all.

Against the backdrop of this very human incident, you and I can examine our feelings of jealousy and discover some secrets about how to cope with them.

Jealousy infects everybody.

All of us, regardless of how good we try to be, experience feelings of jealousy. These feelings began when we were children and envied our playmates' toys. In the full bloom of adulthood, they keep us from enjoying the achievements of our friends. Jealousy plagues us in the sunset years of life when we secretly wish we enjoyed the health of one friend, or the financial security of another.

Centuries ago, a very pious man decided to go into the desert to live as a hermit. He retreated to a cave and spent every waking hour in prayer and meditation. Soon he became famous for his sanctity, and people from far and near came to see the holy hermit. Some of them wanted to distract the hermit from his meditations, so they tried a variety of methods to divert his attention. Friends from the city came and chattered about the latest gossip, but the hermit refused to pay any attention. Others brought delicious food, but the hermit did not touch a morsel. Beautiful women walked by, but he ignored them.

One day the Devil arrived on the scene and saw what was going on. He told the hermit's tormentors, "You aren't subtle enough—let me show you how its done."

He slipped up to the hermit and whispered in his ear, "Your brother has been elected the Bishop of Alexandria." In an instant, a frown clouded the hermit's face and the spell of sanctity was broken.

I have my moments of jealousy, and some of them are related to my vocation as a minister. I know a preacher who has a clever way of taking the major ideas of his sermons and making each of them begin with the same letter of the alphabet. I have tried to do this, but I cannot create that kind of alliteration. Every time I hear him preach, I feel little twinges of jealousy, and a small voice inside me says, "Don't you wish you could do that?"

I have another colleague who is very handsome; the moment he walks into the pulpit, he catches the eye of everyone with his impressive good looks. A mutual friend once said, "He could preach about Mary's little lamb, and a thousand people would say it was the best sermon they had ever heard." That is not fair, because he is a superb preacher, good looks and all. But when I see him or hear him preach, that same little voice inside me says, "Don't you wish you looked like him?" Of course I do!

I am not immune from jealousy, and neither are you. Do you ever see young men or women and wish you were younger? Do you ever think of people who have more money and wish you had their financial resources? Is there someone at your workplace who gets all the breaks, and you feel they are favored? Is there another person who is beautiful, and you are envious because you feel like an ugly duckling? Each of these feelings is a sign that the green-eyed monster is getting hold of you, just as it gets hold of everybody else.

Sigmund Freud, the father of modern psychiatry, was

convinced that jealousy is a normal emotional condition. He also believed that people who think they have no feelings of jealousy are surppressing resentments and trying to work them out at an unconscious level. My own experience as a pastor and as a person confirms that judgment—everyone lives with the curse of jealousy hanging over his or her head.

Jealousy stems from our own insecurities.

In the movie *Snow White and the Seven Dwarfs*, there is a scene in which the queen goes to a secret room to consult a magic mirror. She asks it to name the most beautiful woman in the land. The mirror was supposed to reply that the queen was the fairest, but the magic mirror was uncomprisingly honest. One day it told the queen that Snow White was the most beautiful woman in the realm, and that was when the trouble began.

The queen flew into a rage and began to plan Snow White's destruction; she could not bear to think that someone might be better looking than she was. The jealousy of the queen was the crisis around which the story revolved.

Another classic study of jealousy—created by insecurity—is played out in the movie *Amadeus*. Though music historians doubt the accuracy of the story, it is a classic study of the way jealousy can poison a relationship and destroy people. The plot of the story concerns Antonio Salieri's all-consuming jealousy of Wolfgang Amadeus Mozart. Salieri was court composer to the emperor of Austria, but his music was dull and uninspired.

Mozart was a frivolous, irreverent genius who giggled—nevertheless, he wrote music that angels could sing. When Mozart appeared on the scene in Vienna, he took the city by storm and threatened Salieri's comfortable, mediocre career. For the first time, the court composer was forced to to confront his own inadequacies. Jealousy cankered Salieri's soul and finally drove him to a lunatic asylum; his insecurity in the face of Mozart's genius plagued him until the day he died.

Examine your own feelings. Don't many of your feelings of

jealousy stem from your own insecurities? Mine do; insecurity is a fertile soil in which jealousy can grow. Understanding this dynamic about the green-eyed monster goes a long way toward helping us cope with it.

Our jealousy is our own responsibility.

Lance Webb, in *Conquering the Seven Deadly Sins,* tells about an encounter with a woman on a train. She was sophisticated, well dressed, and beautifully made up, but her spirits were drooping. She had been divorced twice and her third marriage was on the rocks. Unaware that Webb was a clergyman, she shared bits of her philosophy with him.

"Love," she pondered. "What is love?" And without waiting for an answer, she continued:

> Love is a sickly sentiment that puts a romantic wrapping on a shoddy counterfeit. It remains only for a few days until it is discovered to be a sham. . . . If only someone would discover a pill that people could swallow night and morning that would take out all the nasty temper, the venom of envy and green-eyed jealousy, the harsh unkindness, the . . . selfishness and resentment—well, their love could be real and beautiful. Life would be worth living![1]

This disappointed, frustrated woman had an excellent idea—I wish there were a pill all of us could take to help us get rid of our personality flaws, but there is no such remedy. Each of us is responsible for our own inner feelings, broken relationships, and hateful attitudes. As Shakespeare wrote, "Our cures oft within ourselves do lie."

The only way to successfully cope with the green-eyed monster is in the arena of our own hearts. Jealousy cannot be cured from the outside in; it must be cured from the inside out. Were we given all the gifts and graces, advantages and opportunities we admire in others and want for ourselves, within a week we would develop a new list of things to envy. To resolve feelings of jealousy, we must face up to it, analyze it, and then plan a strategy to live beyond it.

Jealousy can be conquered only by serving.

Jesus offered an unusual solution when his friends began to vie for favored places in the Kingdom. He did not chastise them or embarrass them—he called them to be servants: "Whoever wishes to become great among you must be your servant, and whoever wishes to be first among you must be slave of all" (Mark 10:43b-44).

I recently stumbled across a fascinating footnote to history that helped me understand what Jesus was driving at when he talked about people searching for greatness but having to take second place instead. Charles Lindberg made the first trans-Atlantic flight from New York to Paris in 1923. Overnight, the brave young aviator became an international celebrity. Within a month after his heroic adventure, Colonel Lindberg received 3,500,000 letters, 100,000 telegrams, and 14,000 packages. He was offered a fortune for the story of his flight, and hundreds of poems were written in his honor. He was decorated by Congress and almost every country in Europe heaped honors on him. Lindberg remained a romantic figure the rest of his life.

But are you aware that just a few weeks after Lindberg made his historic flight, another American, named Chamberlin, flew across the Atlantic and pushed further east than Paris? Newspapers that bothered to report the story gave it only a few lines on the back page. Mr. Chamberlin had a difficult time persuading the United States government to reimburse even a part of the cost of his flight. He was presented with a few modest decorations by foreign governments, but when he came back to America, he had to pay duty on them.

Insofar as I can determine, Chamberlin never complained. No doubt he must have felt some twinges of jealousy, but he managed to resolve them. He always honored and appreciated Charles Lindberg's trail-blazing flight. Chamberlin was content to live with the knowledge that he too had made a contribution in humankind's effort to conquer the skies, even though he never received adequate recognition.

Perhaps you and I can learn a lesson from this man's experience. Jealousy is a normal human emotion, and none of us can escape it—but each of us can rise above it. The green-eyed monster can be defeated; it is not invincible. But to cope with jealousy, we must be willing to serve and share a part of ourselves with others.

Haunted by a Ghost
Called Yesterday

Putting the Past
into Perspective

Did you know there is a ghost story in the Bible? A lot of folks are not aware of the story, or they have forgotten it, so let me draw a thumbnail sketch of what happened. The time was about 700 years before the birth of Jesus. Saul, a tragic, flawed man, was the first king of Israel. His reign began with great promise, but after a few years he became embroiled in a series of arguments with his neighbors, the Philistines. As a result of stress and political pressure, Saul had a nervous breakdown that made him paranoid.

In the 28th chapter of First Samuel, we meet Saul, lonely and frightened, getting ready to fight the most decisive battle of his life. For years his point of stability, his father figure, had been the prophet Samuel. The prophet had anointed Saul king and tried to advise him about the complexities of government. After his death, Saul felt insecure, exposed, and vulnerable.

As he prepared for battle, the king saw the army of the Philistines camped opposite the forces of Israel, and he panicked. In desperation, Saul convinced himself that he needed to communicate with Samuel. So the night before the battle, he put on a disguise and slipped down to Endor to visit a medium. He pleaded for her to "bring up Samuel for me," which she did (I Sam. 28:11).

But the news was bad—Samuel predicted Saul's defeat. The next day, assuming that he would lose the battle and probably be taken prisoner, Saul took his own life, and his three sons were killed by the Philistines. The battle of Gilboa was a terrible disaster for the Israelites.

Saul's encounter with the medium at Endor is a puzzling story and one may wonder why it was included in the Bible. Perhaps it is there to tell us something about how we should relate to our own past. There are two ways to deal with life's yesterdays: One can honor the past and use it as the basis for building strong traditions. Or one can try to replicate the past and relive it today. The first option is healthy; the second is dangerous. When we attempt to make things like they used to be, we are doomed to defeat as surely as Saul was doomed in the battle that cost him his life.

Nevertheless, all of us, from time to time, ask ourselves why we cannot live in the secure environment of the familiar, rather than deal with the uncertainties of the present and future. To answer this question, let me share some insights I have found helpful in relating yesterday's experiences to today's needs.

Yesterday is not as wonderful as we remember it.

A few years ago, my wife and I spent a delightful weekend in Williamsburg, Virginia. We did all the things tourists usually do in this exquisitely restored colonial town. We visited the governor's mansion, bought hand-crafted items in small shops, and toured several eighteenth-century homes. On Saturday afternoon, a bugle, fife, and drum corps played on the town green. A lot of outdoor cooking was being done, and the aroma of roasting meat was delicious.

I discovered that on Saturday during autumn, people in Williamsburg try to recreate "Market Days" as they were 250 years ago. As I walked around, I could not help thinking, "Wouldn't it have been wonderful to live in a place like this in such an uncomplicated time?"

But do I really want to go back in time and live during the eighteenth century, in Williamsburg or anywhere else?

Consider what life was like then. Life expectancy of the average male was less than sixty years. Women often died in childbirth, and almost every family lost at least one child because the infant mortality rate was extremely high. The faces of many adults were pitted with smallpox scars. When your teeth went bad, they were pulled; then you wore false ones made of wood and ivory. The past, even at Williamsburg, was not as secure as it may have seemed on the surface.

This is also true in our personal experience. Do you sometimes wish you could go back to the safe, secure world of your childhood? I do, and I think about some beautiful lines by Elizabeth Akers:

> Backward, turn backward, O Time, in your flight,
> Make me a child again, just for tonight.

But is that what I want? Not really, because my childhood, like that of most folks, was not nearly as ideal as I remember it. Memory has a beautiful way of blotting out the bad and keeping only the good.

I recall one tragic incident that involved a boy about my age. His name was Billy Smith, and when he was eight or nine, he was stricken with a virulent form of polio. To help him breathe he was confined to an iron lung, where he lay a prisoner for almost ten years before he died. Would I want to go back to a world that had no Salk vaccine, where little children could be paralyzed and die before they had a chance to live?

Even our immediate yesterdays would hardly be called the good old days. The November 1988 issue of *Discover* magazine carried an article that predicted what life will be like in the year 2001. To put things into perspective, the author provided a brief summary of what life was like in 1975. There were few microwave ovens, no VCRs, no residental telephone-answering machines. There was a gasoline shortage looming on the horizon, we were polluting the environment at an alarming rate, and the country was caught in the trauma of Watergate.

Would you like to go back in time and relive that slice of our history? I wouldn't! There is *no* part of my past I want to relive. I have learned that yesterday is not as wonderful as I usually remember it.

Today is not as intimidating as it seems.

A story about a philosophical clock helps me to put some of the pressures of the present into perspective. About a hundred years ago, a clockmaker built a magnificent grandfather clock that not only kept time, but could think as well. Soon after the clock was delivered to its owner, it began to philosophize.

The clock thought, "I am going to tick twice every second. This means that I must tick 120 times a minute, 7,200 times every hour, 172,800 times each day. It also means that I will tick 63,072,000 times in a year!" After making these calculations, the clock collapsed with a nervous breakdown.

The owner returned the clock to the builder for repairs. While the clock was in the shop, it analyzed its problem. Eventually, it reached the conclusion that all it had to do was tick twice each second, and any self-respecting clock could do that much. The rest would take care of itself. Today the philosophical clock is ticking away, keeping perfect time, and it looks as if it will be in mint condition a hundred years from now.

This parable provides a valuable insight about dealing with today's pressures. The given moment often seems frightening when we think about all the tasks we need to accomplish and all the problems we must solve before we go to bed tonight. The best way to deal with these issues is work with them one at a time. It is amazing how much easier things seem when we take one step at a time and trust God for the rest. As the element of trust is injected into the present, the "now" takes on a whole new set of possibilities.

In his book *A View from the Bench*, Judge Joseph A. Wapner, star of television's "The People's Court," tells a story about a case he tried in 1965, when a man named Johnny appeared in his courtroom. Someone back home had convinced Johnny he was handsome enough to be a movie star, so the young man bought a bus ticket and went to Hollywood. He made the rounds of studios, but discovered that nobody was interested. When his money ran out, he had to support himself by washing dishes. One afternoon he hitched a ride with a stranger in what turned out to be a stolen car. Though innocent, Johnny was arrested, booked as an accessory in a car theft, and sent to Judge Wapner's court to be tried.

Johnny's attorney was a perceptive lawyer who knew that his client had not intentionally committed a crime. He made an impassioned argument to the jury, concluding with this statement: "This young man, whom you see before you, has to his name only the pair of jeans he is wearing, his torn white shirt, one pair of shoes, and one pair of socks. His only crime is poverty and ignorance."

The jury acquitted Johnny, then took up money to send him home. Judge Wapner called him to the bench, explained that he was innocent, asked him what size clothes he wore, and asked him to remain in jail over the weekend. The young man must have been puzzled, but he trusted the judge, so he agreed. Over the weekend, the judge went through his own closets, because he and Johnny were the same size, picked out some clothes and collected the boy a new wardrobe. The first thing Monday morning, he presented Johnny with the clothes and sent him on his way to build a new life. This was a happy ending to what could have been a sad episode. It happened because Johnny trusted Judge Wapner, who wanted to help him.[1]

The present can be intimidating—but it is not nearly so frightening when we learn how to trust. We do not need the ghosts of yesterday to get us through today, but we do need a secure relationship with God and trust in one another to help us face the present moment.

The future can be as exciting as we make it.

I once heard a story about a boy who helped pay for his education by selling magazine subscriptions. When he started to work, he decided to call on the president of the university, knowing that a person in such a position would enjoy a wide range of reading. When he rang the doorbell at the president's house, the young man was greeted by the president's wife, who explained that her husband already had more books and magazines than he could read.

When the boy turned to walk away, the president's wife noticed he walked with a limp. Feeling a twinge of guilt, she said, "I'm sorry, I did not know you had a disability."

The student replied that he had polio when he was a boy, so the woman commented, "Having a disability must make a difference in your life."

The young man smiled and said, "Yes, it does, but thank God, I can choose the difference!"

This is where faith intersects the future. You and I cannot always choose what our future will be, but we can choose how we will react to it. We cannot manage events, but we can decide how to handle them.

One of my favorite devotional books is Dag Hammarskjöld's *Markings*. In one passage, he wrote:

> I am being driven forward
> Into an unknown land.
> The pass grows steeper,
> The air colder and sharper.
> A wind from my unknown goal
> Stirs the stirrings
> Of expectation.[2]

Why can't we go back and relive the past? Because the past is not where we ought to be. None of us should be haunted by the ghosts of yesterday; instead, we should listen for the stirrings of expectation in the here and now.

Reach Out and Touch

Developing Sensitivity
in Personal Relationships

I don't pay much attention to television commericals, but there is one I always enjoy. Designed by a telephone company, it tells us to "reach out and touch." The idea is to stay in touch with people we care about by calling them long distance. The people who designed the scenarios for these commercials geared them to fit a variety of situations. In one, a grandchild calls his grandparents. In another, a proud son gets in touch with his parents to tell them about his latest promotion. My favorite features a daughter telephoning her dad, just to tell him she loves him. I also enjoy the one about two women who call each other to relive their college days.

When you analyze these commercials, it is fascinating to think how much the slogan captures a part of the ministry of Jesus, because he was a "toucher." He liked to have hands-on contact with people. He continually touched people—a twelve-year-old girl who was dead; Peter's mother-in-law, sick with a fever; the blind and the deaf; an epileptic; a woman with a twisted back. Jesus also let people touch him—the sick at Gennesaret; the crowds that flocked to hear him; a woman who bathed his feet with her tears; another woman with a hemorrhage of blood; Mary Magdalene, after the resurrection; and "doubting Thomas," who wanted to touch the wounds in his hands, feet, and side.

One of the most dramatic stories about Jesus touching people is told in Mark's Gospel when the writer describes the healing of a leper. He captures the poignancy of the incident in a phrase that tells us quite a bit about why Jesus touched people: "Moved with pity, Jesus stretched out his hand and touched him" (1:41). To understand all the author is implying, we need to know something about how lepers were treated at the time Jesus lived.

In the ancient world, leprosy was a living death which disfigured and mutilated the human body. The disease was highly contagious, so the instant a person was diagnosed with leprosy, he or she was ostracized—cut off from contact with healthy people. Lepers could not enter a city, town, or village. They were required to cry "unclean, unclean," if someone came within shouting distance. They also wore tiny bells sewn into the lining of their clothes, to be sure no one touched them by mistake. Lepers were not supposed to talk to healthy people, because their breath might infect the individual to whom they were speaking.

The leper who came to Jesus violated every law and custom of society in his search for healing. Perhaps he sensed there was something unique about the man from Nazareth, so he pleaded for healing, and he received it. When Jesus touched him, it must have seemed to the leper that he had been reborn.

As the Master's hand touched the leper's deformed, diseased body, the man rediscovered his worth as a person, and in that moment his healing became complete.

The fact that Jesus touched so many people also tells us something about the way we should relate to the persons around us. To share God's presence with others and be a constructive, redemptive force in human relationships, we too must reach out and touch. Touching is a vital part of the way we interact with one another.

Some people are easy to touch.

One Sunday after church, my little grandson came to me, lifted his chubby little arms, and asked to be picked up. I scooped him up, because that is the most natural thing in the world for a grandfather to do. Who can resist touching a grandchild, hugging him, and holding him close?

There is a member of my congregation who comes to the door of the church when services are over, and we always hug each other. I don't remember how this habit started, but now I look forward to my weekly hug. If she is not at worship or I am away from the church, I get two big hugs the next Sunday, to make up for the one I missed the week before. These hugs are important because they are more than a casual embrace; they are an affirmation, a tangible expression of our friendship, as well as a testament of the faith we share.

One morning I was late getting away from the house to go to the church. There was a staff meeting at nine o'clock, and in the rush of leaving, I forgot to kiss my wife good-bye. As I opened the car door, I realized I had missed one of the most important parts of my day. There was no way I was going to face the world without her kiss, so I went back in the house, found her and said, "I forgot something."

In an instant, she knew what it was, and she sent me on my way with a kiss. We reached out and touched each other with the loving ritual of a good-bye kiss which we share every morning.

These touches that are so easy to give and receive may be the level at which you can start reaching out to touch people. They do not frighten or threaten, and they get us in the habit of touching.

Some people are hard to touch.

Christ-like touching is not limited to people who are easy to touch. There are people around us who want to be touched, but they don't know how to express their need, so it's easy to forget to touch them.

If you spend much time around children, you are aware that there is always a shy one in the group. I saw such a child recently. She was a tiny, blond four-year-old, cute as a button, but shrinking back inside her shell. She stood on the fringe of things, her finger in her mouth, looking at the floor, her eyes never quite meeting mine. I knew she desperately wanted to be noticed. I decided to try a smile, a gentle touch, and a few seconds of attention, to see if I could break through her barrier of shyness. I knelt down and took her tiny little hands in mine, asked her name, and started talking to her. In less than five minutes, the little girl wasn't shy anymore; she was chattering so fast I could hardly understand her.

Some adults are like that little girl; they are afraid to let us know how much they crave a touch. If they could tell us how lonely they are and how forgotten they feel, you and I would be shocked. The poem called "Minnie Remembers," from *Mind Song* by Donna Swanson, is a favorite of mine. As I see Minnie in my imagination, she appears a self-sufficent, independent person. But the poet tells another story:

> How long has it been since someone touched me?
> Twenty years?
> Twenty years I've been a widow,
> Respected,
> Smiled at,
> But never touched.
> Never held close to another body,
> Never held so close and warm that loneliness
>   was blotted out.[1]
> (Donna Swanson, Williamsport, Indiana 47993)

Do you know somebody like Minnie—a widow or widower, a divorcee or a single? Or someone with an iceberg for a personality, who comes across as cold and aloof, with barriers so strong you think you could never penetrate them? Reach out and try to touch that person. You may be rebuffed, but keep trying. That person is just like the rest of us inside; he or she desperately wants to be touched, but does not know how to receive the gift.

We are afraid to touch some people.

This is a dimension of touching that is difficult to deal with. I recently read a magazine story about a man and his boss, a

75

woman, who were to go out of town to make a presentation for their company.

The weekend before the trip, the man took his wife on a picnic. That night he began to moan in his sleep, and when his wife awoke, she discovered that he was covered with poison ivy! She rubbed on some lotion, but his business trip was definitely cancelled.

The next morning, his boss came to pick up his part of the presentation they were to make. As he handed her the portfolio, she hesitated and even took a step backward. When she finally accepted the parcel, she held it as far away from herself as possible. She could not bear to shake hands with the swollen, blotchy, rash-covered man standing in front of her. She then made a quick exit—never realizing that poison ivy is not contagious.

Are you like that woman? Sometimes I am—there are people I am afraid to touch. They are dirty or different, they don't smell very good, and they may be contagious. But those are the people who need my touches most.

Time magazine carried a moving story about the visit of Pope John Paul II to the prison cell of Mehmet Ali Agca, the man who tried to assassinate the pope in St. Peter's Square. The report gave a sensitive glimpse of what happened when the two men met for the first time:

> Last week in an extraordinary moment of grace, the violence in St. Peter's Square was transformed. In a bare, white-walled cell in Rome's Rebibbia prison, John Paul tenderly held the hand that held the gun that was meant to kill him. For twenty-one minutes, the two talked softly. Once or twice Agca laughed. The pope forgave him for the shooting. At the end of the meeting, Agca either kissed the pope's ring or pressed the pope's hand to his forehead in a Muslim gesture of respect.[2]

John Paul is the spiritual leader of millions of Roman Catholics and one of the most visible Christians on our planet, but he is also a human being. To take Mehmet Ali Agca's hand, to touch him, must have been one of the most difficult things he ever did. But it was the only gesture that could heal the leprosy of Agca's guilt.

Another beautiful story about the transforming power of a touch is told by Torey Hayden, who teaches disturbed children no one else will deal with. One day a hostile little girl named Shelia was sent to her class. Not long before, Shelia had tied a three-year-old boy to a tree and set fire to him. Her IQ was phenomenal, but Shelia was a terror at school. She punched out the eyes of some goldfish with a pencil, fought with other children, and destroyed more than $700 worth of equipment during a temper tantrum. She would not let anyone touch her, and she refused to be helped.

But Torey Hayden would not give up—she kept reaching out. She fixed Shelia's hair, bathed her, and bought her a new dress. By hugging her, cuddling her, and holding her, Torey helped the little girl learn how to accept love, and to give it. Later, Shelia became a talented and creative woman and wrote a poem for her teacher, titled "To Torey, with Much Love." It ends like this:

> Then you came . . .
> And waited
> Until all my tears turned into
> Joy.

To transform tears into joy, it was necessary for Torey to share the power of a touch with Shelia.[3] To love others as God loves us, we must reach out and touch people. It is not enough to feel sorry for them, pray for them, or sympathize with them—we must *touch* them.

I once read a story about the great religious leaders of the world. It may not be quite fair to other faiths, but it speaks volumes about Christianity.

When a man was caught in a bed of quicksand, Confucius saw him and said, "There is evidence man should stay out of such places."

Buddha saw him and said, "Let that life be a lesson for the rest of the world."

Mohammed said, "It is the will of God."

A Hindu philosopher said, "Do not worry, my friend, you will come back to earth in another form."

But when Jesus saw the man, he said, "Give me your hand, and I will help you out."

"Moved with pity, he stretched out his hand and touched him." Reach out and touch someone—even when that person seems untouchable!

The Delicate Art
of Mending

Healing Broken
Relationships

The seminary I attended occasionally invited senior students to preach in chapel, but those invitations were selective. Each year, only six students were asked to preach. When my last academic year started, I hoped to be selected. The fall quarter passed, then the winter quarter, but no invitation was forthcoming. In early March, the Dean of the chapel asked me to drop by his office. I saw a glimmer of hope, and sure enough, he asked me to preach a couple of weeks before graduation.

I started working on my sermon, studying the text and drawing together material to illustrate some of the ideas I wanted to talk about. Then I remembered—what would I wear? I had only one suit, and after three years in seminary, it was showing signs of severe wear. The place where I carried my billfold was holding together by only a few threads.

I mentioned the problem to my wife, but she said, "John, we can't buy a new suit because we don't have the money. Besides, you will have on a preaching robe, so your suit won't show, new or old." I prayed my suit would survive until the chapel service.

It did not; a couple of weeks before the service, the threads on the back pocket gave way. I panicked—it is one thing to preach in a frayed suit, but quite another to preach with a hole in your trousers, even if they are covered with a robe. My wife, however, is a resourceful woman. The moment I presented her with the worn-out trousers, she got a needle, some thread, and a little scrap of material. And before I knew what was happening, she had mended my trousers so neatly that only a sharp eye could detect the repairs. I was able to preach with my dignity intact!

There are many things that need to be mended. Recently I dropped a piece of fine china and broke it. I carefully gathered up the pieces and took them to a repair shop to be glued back together. A magnificent antique clock that belonged to my grandfather fell off the mantle and was damaged. I picked up the fragments, carried it to a man who restores clocks, and he was able to fix it. When something goes wrong with our car, we take it to a mechanic to be put back in good running order. Even our bodies become sick and need to heal or be healed. We are continually repairing broken things, but our most delicate task of mending deals not with objects but relationships. Jesus dealt with this issue during the Sermon on the Mount:

> When you are offering your gift at the altar, if you remember that your brother or sister has something against you, leave your gift there before the altar and go; first be reconciled to your brother or sister, and then come and offer your gift. (Matt. 5:23-24)

To understand what Jesus was saying, we need to know that sacrifice was an important part of Hebrew ritual. If someone wronged another, that person also disturbed his or her relationship with God. To set matters right, a sacrifice was offered to mend the divine-human relationship. Jesus carried the matter a step further: To heal a broken relationship with God, we must mend our fractured relationships with one another.

This profound insight is as valid today as it was two thousand years ago. Because the healing process is sometimes complex, I want to suggest some ways we can mend our broken relationships with the people around us.

Identify the cause of the break.

Before any relationship can be healed, we need to understand what caused the break in the first place. There are a variety of reasons for relationships getting out of kilter. One reason is neglect—we often lose friends because we do not nurture our friendships. A friend of mine recently headed a large building project in a major city. I was proud of what he was doing, and I received regular reports about the progress of the building program. Just a few weeks before the building was finished, I realized I had not written him to tell him how proud I was of all he had accomplished. Fortunately, I rectified my omission—but there was a possibility that my insensitivity could have cooled our friendship.

Marriages often break apart because one or both spouses forget to nurture their relationship with little acts of kindness—a quick kiss, a gentle touch, a loving smile. Neglect has destroyed more marriages, ruined more friendships, and broken more relationships that any other single thing.

On occasion, we also make unintentional blunders that can fracture a relationship before we know what has happened. One Sunday after church my wife and I were having lunch with a friend who was wearing a stunning dress.

Thinking I was paying her a compliment, I said, "Your dress is lovely; it is one of my favorites. I've noticed you wearing it several times the last few weeks, and I have admired it each time. It is a beautiful dress."

She responded with a tight little smile and said quietly, "Thank you, John."

I happened to glance across the table at my wife, who had an "I wish I could stuff your tongue" expression on her face. Later when we were alone, she explained my blunder: "John, when you compliment a woman on what she is wearing, there is no need to comment on how often she has worn it."

Fortunately, my faux pas did not rupture our friendship, but it could have. All of us have inadvertantly or unknowingly hurt people of whom we are fond. The price of our mistakes has been a threat to the relationship.

81

Fear can also destroy a relationship. I heard of a young woman who had been tragically widowed at age thirty, but who eventually started dating again. She was an intelligent, attractive, vibrant person with a good job, but after a few dates, men would drop her. She went to a counselor to find out why. When the two of them gently sorted through her emotions, they discovered the problem. At one level, this young woman thought she wanted to marry again, but down deep, she was frightened that she would lose another mate. She unconsciously said and did things to keep men at a distance. Her fear was destroying any possibility for remarriage.

We must not forget that relationships are often broken because people do spiteful and hateful things to each other. Ugly, unfair words or intentional acts that hurt create breaches in relationships that are almost impossible to resolve. Nevertheless, when we are mean-spirited, we should own up to our dark side and try to repair the damage we have done.

To mend a relationship, you need to begin the healing process by identifying the cause of the break.

Let the miracle of forgiveness work.

Broken relationships cannot be healed without forgiveness. Each party must show compassion, acceptance, and understanding. Forgiveness is the glue that binds people back together after a relationship has been broken.

I grew up during World War II, and one of my favorite games was "war." My best friend's name was Ben, and during one such game we found ourselves on opposite sides. As in real life, the longer the game went on, the more the hostilities escalated.

One of the older boys on my side said, "Johnny, you crawl up to the front line and call Ben a _____." I had no idea what the word meant, so I shouted the insult at the top of my lungs. In an instant, I ruptured my friendship with Ben.

We did not speak to each other for several weeks. I was miserable, and my father, guessing something was wrong between us, asked what the problem was. I told him about the incident during the game, and Dad responded with two comments. First he said never to call anybody that again. Then he told me to go to Ben and apologize.

I went to Ben's house that afternoon, walked across his front porch, and rang the doorbell. When Ben came to the door, he was surprised to see me, but before he could say a word, I blurted out my apology:

"Ben, I'm sorry I called you a nasty name. I didn't know what it meant."

He grinned and said, "Johnny, it's OK. I figured you didn't know what you were saying." And because the miracle of forgiveness had done its work, five minutes later we were playing together as if nothing had happened.

The same miracle can happen in adult relationships. Leo Buscaglia pays a beautiful tribute to a friend who died not too long before he wrote *Bus 9 to Paradise*. He explains how he and his friend nurtured their relationship, gave each other room to make mistakes, and supported each other in failure. Then he makes a beautiful statement:

> We hurt or disappointed each other from time to time, but from this we learned to practice the delicate art of human forgiveness until we reached the point where we could look beyond the hurt rather than backward in anger and resentment. We stopped judging and censuring. We knew that when the other was foolish or had lapses, it was never a permanent condition.[1]

Buscaglia's phrase, "the delicate art of human forgiveness," says it all. Relationships cannot be healed without forgiveness. When we let the gentle power of forgiveness do its work, healing and reconciliation inevitably follow.

Heal the wound while there's still time.

One of the crucial elements in any relationship is timing. We need to know when to laugh or cry with each other, when to hug or keep our distance, when to speak and when to be

83

silent. But the most crucial dimension is knowing when to heal—and the time is always *now.*

Alan Loy McGinnis, a Christian psychiatrist and counselor, tells about a man who came to him with a problem of depression. Dr. McGinnis asked whether the man and his wife had any close friends.

The fellow replied, "Nope. We speak to our neighbors, but we never have anybody in," and then he explained why. Ten years before, he and his wife had been close to another couple. They played cards, went out socially, and even took a vacation together. But suddenly the other couple terminated the friendship.

Apparently the depressed man had said something that offended his friends. But he had refused to pursue the problem because, "If they are going to get upset like that, what's the use?" So a friendship was fractured but never mended.

Dr. McGinnis said, "I find that a very, very sad story."[2]

That *is* a sad story, because it happens frequently. Friendships that could be salvaged and relationships that could be mended are never healed because people let them disintegrate. They do not mend them while there is still time.

A young woman wrote a beautiful poem, "Things You Didn't Do," about her friend. Her words speak for themselves:

> Remember the day I borrowed your brand new car and I
>   dented it?
> I thought you'd kill me, but you didn't.
> And remember the time I dragged you to the beach, and you
>   said it would rain, and it did?
> I thought you'd say, "I told you so." But you didn't.
> Do you remember the time I flirted with all the guys to make
>   you jealous, and you were?
> I thought you'd leave me, but you didn't.
> Do you remember the time I spilled strawberry pie all over
>   your car rug?
> I thought you'd hit me, but you didn't.
> And remember the time I forgot to tell you the dance was
>   formal and you showed up in jeans?

I thought you'd drop me, but you didn't.
Yes, there were lots of things you didn't do.
But you put up with me, and you loved me, and you protected
  me.
There were lots of things I wanted to make up to you when you
  returned from Viet Nam.
But you didn't.[3]

Are you concerned about a friendship that isn't what it used to be? Are you part of a relationship that has lost its excitement and sparkle? Have you hurt someone and don't know how to say "I'm sorry"? Has someone hurt you and you are afraid to take the first step toward reconcilation? Is a secret pain eating away at your heart because someone you love has bruised it?

Mend it—while there's still time!

Another Shot
at Life

Living
Without Regrets

Some time ago I stumbled across part of a column by Erma Bombeck, with the intriguing title, "If I Had My Life to Live Over."

The point of the column is that there are so many things she would do differently, if she could have another chance at life. She would express her love more frequently, her regrets more openly, and really live life to the fullest.

I suspect you have some of the same feelings Ms. Bombeck described, because most of us, if given another shot at life, would do many things differently.

When I look back across my life, I would change several things, if I could. To begin with, I would learn how to spell better. When I was a youngster, I enjoyed school, but I hated spelling. I loved to read but couldn't be bothered to take time to learn how to arrange the letters in their correct sequence. Today I am paying the price for my childhood neglect; when I write, I sit with a dictionary at my elbow, and someone has to carefully check every sentence before it is typed.

If I could start over, I would also pay more attention to friendships and not allow them to lapse because of neglect. During the Christmas season I received a card from a person to whom my wife and I were very close twenty-five years ago. Enclosed was a clipping announcing the death of her father the preceding October. These folks were good to my family and me when I was preparing for the ministry, and for several years we stayed in close contact. But time passed, my responsibilities grew, and before I knew what was happening, our relationship had withered. When I read the obituary, I wished that I had nurtured our friendship to keep it vibrant and alive. Perhaps you have a similar regret—there are so many things each of us would do differently if we had a chance.

A fascinating story in the Bible tells about someone who had a chance to relive one event in his life and rectify a mistake. The incident is recorded in John's Gospel, and the passage is often called "The Restoration of Simon Peter" (John 21:15-19). To understand the meaning of the story, we should project it against the background of an event that happened before Jesus was crucified.

On the night Jesus was being tried for his life, Simon Peter was standing in the courtyard of the high priest's house. When someone asked Peter if he was a follower of Jesus, Peter denied that he even knew Jesus. He was asked the same question a second time, then a third, and each time, he swore vehemently that he did not know the man from Galilee. Then a rooster crowed, and Peter realized he had denied his best friend when he needed him most (John 18:25-28).

But that is not the end of the story. After his resurrection, Jesus had breakfast with his disciples beside the Sea of Galilee. While they were eating, he asked Peter, "Simon son of John, do you love me more than these?" When Peter replied that he loved Jesus with all his heart, Jesus posed the question again. The third time Jesus asked the question, Peter probably was irritated, so he may have almost shouted, "Lord, you know everything; you know that I love you" (John 21:17). At that point, perhaps Peter realized what was happening—Jesus was giving him a chance to start over, to answer the question differently. Though he could never erase the fact of his denial, he could always cherish the memory of his restoration.

I have often wondered what I would do differently if I were

given a chance to amend the past. Many possibilities flash across my consciousness—but four changes would be at the top of my list. These four priorities are the keys to living without regrets.

Learn to express your feelings more creatively.

Several years ago I dropped by my doctor's office with a bad cold, feeling wretched. When he came into the examining room and asked, "John, how are you feeling?" I straightened up, tried to put on my brightest smile, and replied, "Fine, and how are you?"

Since the doctor was a close friend, he chuckled and answered, "I'm fine—but if you're feeling so good, what are you doing here?" Unknowingly, he had identified a problem many of us have: We wear masks to hide what is really going on inside us.

Some feelings, such as love and anger, are easy to express. One of my nicest Christmas presents was from one of my daughters—an enlargement of a picture of me holding my grandaughter. A glance at the photograph will tell you exactly what I was feeling when it was taken—I was the proudest grandfather in the world! Nor do I keep my anger a secret. I am one of those who, when angry, get mad all over. I am able to control my frustrations most of the time, but when they explode, they errupt like a volcano.

The feelings I have a problem sharing are my hurts, anxieties, and fears. I suspect that if you are candid, you may have this problem too. William Miller, in *The Joy of Feeling Good*, relates the story of a woman who went to a psychiatrist because she was severely depressed. As her therapist began to probe her emotions, he discovered she had never worked through the death of her husband many years before. Her husband had died one week after President Kennedy was assassinated. She had watched with admiration how well Mrs. Kennedy handled the shock and trauma of her husband's death, and when her own husband died, she made up her mind to be just as composed, calm, and brave, saying

ANOTHER SHOT AT LIFE

to herself, "If Jackie Kennedy can do it, so can I." She did not realize that Jackie Kennedy on national television was not Jackie Kennedy behind the scenes, sharing her heartbreak with her family and friends. So that woman's grief remained repressed because she never let herself express what she was really feeling.[1]

To be whole and healthy, we must learn to communicate what is going on inside us, even when it is painful to do so. Feelings that are repressed remain unresolved emotional issues—especially if we are nursing them as secret hurts, resentments, or disappointments.

In *Everything to Gain*, Jimmy and Rosalynn Carter talked about some of their bruised feelings and how they lived beyond them. Rosalynn described how the two of them tried to cope with her husband's defeat for a second term in 1980. She remembered how well-meaning friends would say, "Don't you worry about the election. You're about to start on the most exciting part of your life."

Wrote Rosalynn Carter, "That was not true, it would never be true and we'd rather not hear people say it. . . . We'd thrived even with the criticisms, and we loved politics. . . . We appreciated our friends' concern, but there was just no way they could know how we were really feeling."[2]

Being this honest in print must have been a theraputic experience for the Carters, which helped to heal some of the wounds of their defeat.

If I could start over, I would be as candid about my emotions as Rosalynn Carter has been. It is healthy to be open and expressive with all our feelings—especially the ones we try to hide from public view.

Be more focused in the present.

I was reminded of the importance of focusing on the present when my wife decided to go into the travel business. The owner of a successful travel agency gave her a piece of advice: Always remember that people enjoy planning a trip as much as they enjoy taking one, because a travel experience begins when a client decides to go.

Eventually, my wife became an experienced travel counselor and a partner in her own agency. She discovered how right her friend was; when people made reservations for a trip, they enjoyed studying maps, reading brochures, and learning as much as they could about the area they planned to visit. When clients came to her office to make their travel arrangements, she usually loaded them down with material—and she had a lot of repeat business because of the thorough way she helped her customers prepare for their trips. Life's most delectable moments are not yesterday or tomorrow, but *now.* Creative living is centered in the present, not in the past or the future.

A friend of mine once told a group of pastors about some advice his father had given him at the beginning of his career. My friend had read a beautiful story that could help to illuminate a profound idea in a sermon, so he jotted down some notes, filed the story away, and told his father, who was also a preacher, about it. The father asked my friend whether he was going to tell the story the next Sunday.

My friend replied, "Papa, I'm saving the story for a special day like Easter."

"Don't do that," his father advised. "Use it next Sunday. Give every week's sermon the best you've got, and God will take care of the rest."

This is sound advice both for preaching and for living. Focus on the now—don't live in the past or hold back for the future—give the present the best you have. If I could live a part of my life over, I would spend less time regretting what happened yesterday or being concerned about what might happen tomorrow. I would try to enjoy every moment of today, because that's where the action is.

Be more sensitive to the feelings of others.

I heard about a woman who took her son Christmas shopping because she thought he would have a wonderful time looking at holiday decorations, seeing window displays, watching animated toys, and so forth. After a few minutes the youngster began to fret and cry; then one of his shoelaces came untied and he started tripping over his own feet.

As she bent down to tie his shoe, his mother said in exasperation, "I brought you with me to get the Christmas spirit!" But as she was tying his shoe, she saw the department store from the perspective of a five-year-old, as her son saw it. From his view, there were no lights, decorations, holiday garlands, or animated toys. All the little boy could see was a maze of aisles and the legs of people running here and there. When his mother saw reality as the child saw it, her relationship with him changed—she became sympathetic and understanding.

If I could start over, I would try to remember that mother's experience as I relate to people every day. It is so easy to deal with people from my own narrow perspective that I tend to forget their hurts, needs, anxieties, and fears.

One rainy winter morning, my telephone rang at 7:00, while I was drinking my first cup of tea. The man on the line was frantic because he was being evicted from his apartment. For a few seconds, I felt a wave of impatience—there was nothing I could do to help him at that hour.

Then, as I sat in the snug, warm, cosy security of my breakfast nook, I asked myself, "How would you feel if you had no place to go on a cold, wet, dreary Friday morning?" Suddenly it dawned on me that this man wasn't calling me to do something; he was calling because he needed a friend, somebody to talk to, someone to sympathize with him.

When people around us hurt, most of them just want a friend to listen, a shoulder to cry on, a person who understands. They want someone to sympathize, share their hurts, and respond to their emotional needs. Think about those needs the next time you encounter a person who is living through a painful episode. Your sensitivity will help that person and prevent you from later wishing you had responded differently.

Give more of yourself to others.

The Giving Tree, by Shel Silverstein, is the story of a tree that loves a little boy. He gathers her leaves, climbs her

91

trunk, swings from her branches, and eats the apples she grows. The boy loves the tree as much as she loves him, but when he grows older, he stops climbing and playing in the tree. But the tree doesn't mind; she tells him to gather her apples, take them to the city, and sell them.

Several years pass, and the tree gives her branches to help build the boy a house. Finally she surrenders her trunk so that he can make a boat. By this time, there is nothing left of the Giving Tree but a stump. When the boy, now an old man, comes back to visit, the tree apologizes because she has no apples, no branches, not even a trunk. But he explains that he doesn't need any of those things, so the tree offers all she has left—her stump.

"Come, Boy, sit down. Sit down and rest," she said.

And the story ends with two brief but beautiful sentences: "And the boy did. And the tree was happy."[3]

The parable of the Giving Tree speaks for itself—we are happiest when we give ourselves to others. Sometimes we can give much; at other times, only a little. But whatever we can give blesses us at least as much as it blesses those with whom we share. Don't hold tightly to too much of yourself—someday you may wish you had given away more.

Do you wish you had another shot at life? Of course—all of us do. We know we can't relive the past. But we can begin where we are, and start living now, so that someday we will have no regrets.

Notes

Narcissus Is More Than a Flower

1. Cecil Osborne, *The Art of Understanding Yourself* (Grand Rapids: Zondoveran Publishing House, 1967), pp. 166-67.
2. Alan Loy McGinnis, *Confidence: How to Succeed at Being Yourself* (Minneapolis: Augsburg Publishing House, 1987), pp. 28-29.
3. Robert Schuller, *Self Esteem: The New Reformation* (Irving, Tex.: Word, Inc., 1982), pp. 91-92.

What Does God Look Like?

1. Wallace Hamilton, *Who Goes There?* (Westwood, N. J.: Fleming H. Revell, 1958), pp. 11-12.
2. John Gillespie Magee, Jr., "High Flight," *One Thousand Beautiful Things*, comp. Majorie Barrows (New York: Spencer Press, 1957), p. 22.
3. Mervyn Warren, "Suppose God is Black," *Best Sermons*, ed. James W. Cox and Kenneth M. Cox (San Francisco: Harper & Row, 1988), pp. 242-43.

Guess Who Came to the Sparrow's Funeral?

1. Earl Hunt, *I Have Believed* (Nashville: The Upper Room, 1980), p. 32.
2. James Gordon Gilkey, *There Is Help for You* (New York: Macmillan Publishing Co., 1951), p. 141.
3. "Look, God," by Michael Schafernocker, cited in Charles L. Allen, *In Quest of God's Power* (Westwood, N. J.: Fleming H. Revell, 1986), pp. 174-75.

Wisdom from a Sandbox

1. Robert Fulghum, *All I Really Need to Know I Learned in Kindergarten* (New York: Random House, 1988), pp. 6 ff.

NOTES

2. Walter J. Burghardt, *Still Proclaiming Your Wonders* (New York: Paulist Press, 1984), p. 168.

Whistle While You Work

1. James Gordon Gilkey, *There Is Help for You* (New York: Macmillian Publishing Co., 1951), p. 21.
2. Charles Colson (with Elen Santilli Vaughn), *Kingdoms in Conflict* (Grand Rapids: Zondervan Publishing House, 1987), pp. 67-68.
3. Warren I. Susman, *Culture as History: The Transformation of American Society in the Twentieth Century* (New York: Pantheon Books, 1985), p. 136.

Defeating the Green-eyed Monster

1. Lance Webb, *Conquoring the Seven Deadly Sins* (Nashville: Abingdon Press, 1955), p. 56.

Haunted by a Ghost Called Yesterday

1. Joseph A. Wapner, *A View from the Bench* (New York: Penguin Books, 1987), p. 33ff.
2. Dag Hammarskjöld, *Markings*, trans. Leif Sjöberg and W. H. Auden (New York: Alfred A. Knopf, 1964), p. 5.

Reach Out and Touch

1. Donna Swanson, "Minnie Remembers," *Images*, comp. Janice Grana (Nashville: The Upper Room, 1976), p. 118.
2. *Time*, January 9, 1984, p. 28.
3. Walter J. Burghardt, *Seasons That Laugh and Weep* (New York: Paulist Press, 1983), p. 28 ff.

The Delicate Art of Mending

1. Leo Buscaglia, *Bus 9 to Paradise*, ed. Daniel Kimbler (Thorofare, N. J.: Slack, Inc., 1986), p. 17.
2. Alan Loy McGinnis, *Confidence: How to Succeed at Being Yourself* (Minneapolis: Augsburg Publishing House, 1987), pp. 146-47.
3. Leo Buscaglia, *Living, Loving, and Learning*, ed. Steven Short (New York: Fawcett, 1982), p. 76.

Another Shot at Life

1. Edward Paul Cohn, "Go Ahead and Grow," cited in *Best Sermons*, ed. James W. Cox (San Francisco: Harper & Row, 1988), p. 381.
2. Jimmy Carter and Rosalynn Carter, *Everything to Gain: Making the Most of the Rest of Your Life* (New York: Random House, 1987), p. 13.
3. Shel Silverstein, *The Giving Tree* (New York: Harper & Bros., 1964).